Let's Work Together

Let's Work Together

Nathan Wright, Jr.

Hawthorn Books, Inc.   *Publishers*   New York

First Edition: 1968
Second Paperback Printing: 1968
Third Paperback Printing: 1969
Second Hardcover Printing: 1969

ACKNOWLEDGMENTS

"Let America Be America Again," copyright 1938 by Langston Hughes. Renewed. Reprinted by permission of Harold Ober Associates.

"Negro Leader Critical of White Friends" by Ralph McGill. Reprinted by permission of *The Atlanta Constitution*.

"Education is Fuel for Economic Fires" by Sylvia Porter. Courtesy of Publishers-Hall Syndicate.

Material from "The Gift of Blackness" by Vincent Harding is reprinted from Katallagete—Be Reconciled, The Journal of Southern Churchmen, Box 12044, Nashville, Tennessee.

Material from "The Road to Racial Irrelevance in America" by Margaret Mead © 1968 by The New York Times Company.

Contents

To
My twin, Benjamin Hickman Wright,
a constant resource and a brother,
and to
Lina Louise Wright Fleming and
Lydia Turah Wright Evans,
my sisters

CHAPTER ONE

Are We Really Together?

RECENTLY I VISITED THE RETIRED RECTOR OF ST. ANDREW'S Episcopal Church in Cincinnati, Ohio, the parish in which I grew up. Father and Mrs. Edmund Oxley, both now in their eighties, are a gracious and delightful couple. Throughout his ministry of more than fifty years in his adopted Cincinnati, Father Oxley, a native West Indian, had been conservative in his political and social outlook. His brilliant mind and his conservatism had won him the confidence of those with power in the city. Any member of the black community who needed a job or wanted a favor could turn to Father Oxley with confidence that, if it were at all possible to open a door for a black person, he was the one who could do it. When I was growing up in St. Andrew's parish, I used to hear Father Oxley speak of the many fine white people who were the black men's friends. I became accustomed to the notion that black men's growth to maturity and freedom depended largely upon white benevolence, and my feelings have been shared by countless others.

Yet Father Oxley is representative of an earlier era, in which black and white Americans sought a form of toleration and accommodation. And he tends to view the present in terms of the past as he experienced it. His mind is still amazingly alert and his speaking voice precise and resonant as he declares to public gatherings that "the power structure of our city is sound!"

Mrs. Oxley, who is in many ways her husband's opposite, gently chides him in private: "Now Father, remember your day is past. The younger people today have the opportunity to deal with reality far better than we could." Then, Mrs. Oxley, whose natural charm is enhanced by her perennial youthfulness and nobility of spirit, declares: "I am proud that I am a militant. I just bubble over inside when I see young people today who have pride in being what they are and who are determined to make their life better than our generation either could or would."

There is more to the story of the Oxleys, but the part told here bespeaks a significant and growing trend in relations between black and white Americans. And few of his listeners, although they respect him personally, can take Father Oxley's message seriously today, for they know that even the past was never really what he remembers it as having been.

The terms "cooperation" and "interracial" have long been used for relations that are neither cooperative nor interracial. Every black community in the United States, north or south, has had its Father Oxley, its conservative spokesman recognized by those in power. Usually a man with professional training, probably in the ministry or in medicine, he has helped to ease the guilt of the white community and to perpetuate the myth that black men can indeed, merely by following the rules, achieve success in the world as it is presently structured. The white community's preferential treatment of chosen black men has given apparent substance to the claim of interracial cooperation and has helped it to disguise from itself the ways in which it keeps the total black community in check. On the national level too, statesmen have been elected, by white and black men together, who have made genuine efforts to influence the consciences of white men and the white institutions that control the destinies of black men.

Yet, from the very nature of these efforts at interracial cooperation, it is clear that relations between black and white men have been neither interracial nor cooperative. Instead, what has been called "cooperation between the races" has consisted of black people's adherence to an agenda and a set of principles established mainly by white people.

The atmosphere in the United States even today recalls the ethos of slavery. Power over black lives remains in the hands of white people. The voices of black men do not command respect, for they still speak as powerless men through leaders who must first be accepted by those in power before they can be heard.

Under such circumstances genuine interracial cooperation can hardly exist. Many among us who once hoped to bring it about have had a rude awakening. Reflecting the character of Americans as a whole, black Americans have tended to be idealistic in their quest for equality, sometimes recklessly so. And from the head-on collision of this reckless idealism with harsh reality, black militance is born. Sometimes we forget that Stokely Carmichael was once an optimistic, even a starry-eyed, crusader. To many who have known him since those days, he is the nation's most obvious casualty of the deadly confrontation of hope and intransigent denial.

Stokely Carmichael is the embodiment—in some respects almost a caricature—of an impatient new generation, black and white. Because the needs of this nation have changed and recognition of those needs has not kept pace, Stokely's tribe seems certain to increase. The growing restlessness of young people in general and the deliberate repressive measures against black people in our cities are signs of the necessity for change on one hand and unwillingness to accept change on the other. It is ironic—tragically so—that a society whose success has always seemed rooted in its adaptability should seek to freeze its social arrangements just at that moment when the need for adaptability presses most heavily upon it, when pressure for social change has become a global force. White Americans have tended to close ranks or to concede only minimal, token adjustments at a time when aggressive action to secure equity for black Americans should be their most pressing commitment. And on those occasions when the weight of world opinion and violent discord at home have at last forced us to confront the needs of black Americans with sincere purpose, our best efforts have fallen short of the needs of the hour.

Not long ago I was delayed at the airport of one of our great cities. As I waited, I saw evidence of a condition in the airline industry that is typical of the American economy as a whole: a highly disproportionate number of white employees at upper levels and relatively few black employees, practically all of them in lower-echelon jobs. Despite the availability of qualified applicants, there are very few black pilots working in the United States. The higher-paid clerical, supervisory, and managerial categories in the aviation industry also reflect a serious failure to achieve equitable employment for black people.

The airport was situated far from the center of the city, and new houses were springing up all around it, despite the growing nuisance of airport noise. I asked myself what kind of people were coming to live there, and the answer, of course, was white people seeking to escape from city problems and from the black people with whose arrival they associate those problems. Both industry and the white population have been moving out of the cities just as those black people who are best qualified for industrial and service jobs are moving from regions of low economic opportunity into the cities. Yet the black people cannot follow the industrial and service jobs into the suburbs, for most suburban communities exclude them both overtly and covertly. That more and more black Americans cannot live where work is available is causing growing desperation among them and a dangerous situation for the nation as a whole.

There has been much talk recently of polarization between white and black Americans. The assumption is that black people have retreated from a cooperative spirit and an integrated approach to betterment of their condition. The opposite is nearer the truth. For it is the white Americans who have been reluctant to cooperate with black men on equal terms, who refuse to relinquish their direct power over black men's lives. This attitude is not surprising, for history offers few instances of power freely shared. Nor *can* power, in fact, be given freely. Implicit in the free grant of power by one group to another is the ability to take it away as freely, and therefore what is being transmitted is not power but a more subtle form of dependence. Only through striving for and seizing power is the muscle necessary to use and maintain it developed.

The servile or dependent attitude that was, for a period, necessary to the survival of black people in the United States is incompatible with the development by black people of the power to control their own destinies. Even when white people have sincerely sought self-sufficiency for black people, persistent black preoccupation with survival has worked against the achievement of power.

Polarization has existed, then, for some time. Its recent acceleration is rooted in continuing inequitable relationships of power. This condition has been seriously aggravated by a general failure of spirit throughout the nation.

As early as the 1920s, the United States had begun to

move away from its pioneering past, at least in social terms. Cities had been built. Railroads crisscrossed the land. Huge profits were already being made. It was possible to believe that an adolescent nation, through its rescue of the world powers in World War I, had come of age and had proved itself a master in, if not yet of, the world. In the postwar era, there was a consensus that the nation had "arrived." The rapid expansion of the Ku Klux Klan during the 1920s was one reflection of national satisfaction with the status quo—an unwillingness any longer to tolerate the kind of social receptiveness that had in fact helped to shape the nation's greatness. Few well-intentioned people in those days opposed the work of the Klan.

During the Great Depression of the 1930s, emphasis shifted to the fight for survival on a national scale. In an era when recovery was the paramount need, there was no time to think of going forward; indeed, the kind of social change that most men sought was a return to the "good old days."

During and after World War II, however, the nation began to make new affirmations of the democratic ideal. Franklin Delano Roosevelt's executive order establishing fair employment practices—a response to black discontent over wartime employment inequities—ensured maximum efficiency in the use of American manpower at a critical time. Immediately after the war, the Full Employment Act of 1946, potentially the most significant—though still largely unused—social legislation of our time was passed. It empowered the Federal government to adopt all possible means to ensure full use of the nation's employment resources. Implementation of this legislation may yet one day provide economic opportunity for all.

In the booming postwar economy, there was a widespread conviction that the economic condition of black people was improving. As the nation moved precipitously from a mixed farm-and-factory economy to one characterized by modern technology and automation, more black people entered the traditional white-collar occupations. That this trend reflected a broad change in the economy, rather than substantial racial progress, remained largely unrecognized, however. Indeed, until 1952, postwar prosperity seemed to promise that at long last the economic gap between white and black Americans would close.

The apparent connection between legislation and economic success encouraged the belief that legislation was also the key to long-denied civil rights and social opportunities for Negroes. The Supreme Court's school-desegregation decision in 1954 was widely hailed as a milestone in opening doors, at least legally, to schools formerly closed to black children.

I had taken part in the first freedom ride, the Journey of Reconciliation, which was sponsored by the Congress of Racial Equality in 1947. Its intention was to test the 1945 Supreme Court decision, in the Irene Morgan case, providing for desegregation of all interstate travel. Such travel did slowly become integrated, but carriers in the South still relegated black people to inferior status, requiring them to sit in the rear of public conveyances. The spirit of that first freedom ride was revived ten years later in Montgomery, Alabama, when Mrs. Rosa Parks refused to move to the rear of a bus. Her refusal and the subsequent involvement of the late Dr. Martin Luther King gave rise to what came to be known as the "freedom movement." This great effort—unprecedented in the nation's history—was marked by sit-ins, kneel-ins, freedom marches, freedom rallies, freedom rides, freedom songs, freedom schools, and a powerful drive for legislative guarantees of everything that comes under the label "freedom," culminating in the 1963 March on Washington.

Dr. Anna Arnold Hedgeman, undoubtedly one of the foremost contributors to our recent racial progress, has made a sobering assessment of all those efforts:

From the time of my service as Executive Director of the National Council for a Fair Employment Practices Commission in 1943 until 1967, I have been a part of most of the major endeavors in the Negro's struggle for freedom. The nature of my employment, which I always took a large part in shaping, gave me an almost unparalleled entree into and opportunity to promote support for efforts at breaking what were thought to be the last barriers of prejudice and discrimination.

I found myself working soberly and reflectively. Yet during the decade following 1957 our bi-racial leadership was often caught up in the enthusiasm of the hour. Our basic mistake during this later period —when the Freedom Movement became almost a sacred thing—was our failure to test carefully our planning as to whether we were actually achieving our hoped-for goals. My experience with Fair Employment Practices had taught me that the struggle for freedom cannot be properly evaluated in moments of great enthusiasm.

Nonetheless, at the March on Washington itself, I knew that this was a mood which, if utilized properly, might proceed to more realistic basic planning. In 1964 after the passage of the Civil Rights Bills, I again hoped that the mood of participation and achievement might be stimulated toward the recognition of the necessity for change in our community structures to provide proper relationships for capital development.

In 1965, I proposed a conference of Negro and white leadership which would renew already established programs in both the north and the south. The refusal of significant forces to listen to Negroes who urged critical planning and evaluation; the determination to develop a kind of missionary program for Negroes; the failure to consult with Negroes with experience and know-how led to an alarming and perilous condition.

Desperation and fury, fed by indifference and a callous return to the *status quo*, resulted in the negation of the goals of the black man.

Black people who had entered the freedom movement with starry-eyed optimism and supreme dedication were appalled at the signs of desperation in the black community after 1965. This desperation mounted despite the increased commitment of the nation—including the leadership role of whites in black affairs—to racial progress. Although the avowed goal of the nation was to close the social and economic gap between white and black Americans, the gap was in fact not even narrowing. Indeed, it was estimated that, at the rate of improvement in urban education in 1967, it would take seventy years to close the educational gap between the races! The dollar-income gap has shown no clear sign of disappearing over the past decade. In 1954, at the time of the school-desegregation decision, there were 2.2 million black children in all-black schools; in 1967 the figure was 2.5 million. Was "progress" being made? There are growing doubts among black people that either moderation or cooperation with white people is the pathway to freedom or even to racial progress. Roy Wilkins, the amiable, deeply dedicated, but cautious executive secretary of the National Association for the Advancement of Colored People, spoke at his organization's 1967 convention in Boston of the need to question moderation as an approach. Other voices have also been raised. Ralph McGill, in a syndicated

column entitled "Negro Leader Critical of White
Friends," recounts the thinking of Dr. Benjamin Mays,
long one of the most esteemed pleaders of the black cause
before white Americans:

> Dr. Benjamin E. Mays, who came a long road
> from a tenant farm in an obscure area of South Caro-
> lina to a lengthy span of useful and distinguished
> years as president of Morehouse College is now pres-
> dent emeritus. But occasionally he holds and teaches
> a "class."
> There is no bitterness in him. There is a generous
> residue of that stubborn determination that enabled
> him to build a small Negro college into a strong and
> growing one and himself into a nationally known
> educator. That there is no bitterness is an eloquent
> tribute to his civilized intelligence and humanity.
> He knew humiliations. They may be illustrated. He
> once was slapped and cuffed as a young teenager by
> an arrogant small-town "rich man." He was once
> driven from a Pullman berth by two pistol-pointing
> passengers who, with no authority, ordered him out.
> These are but two of many episodes.
> The present is a time of learning, of adjustment,
> and of change. Dr. Mays discusses those "liberal
> friends" who will "dine and wine with us in the
> swankiest hotels, and work with us, but who still
> discriminate when it comes to money and power."
> Such "liberals," he believes, "are more of a problem
> than the clearly delineated Wallaces, Barnetts, Mad-
> doxes, and Williamses."
> This statement may be obscure even to persons
> of the best of will and wish. It may be clarified by a
> further observation under the general heading of
> "power."

"For a long time," he says, "the wealth of this nation will be in the hands of white Americans, and not Negroes. Therefore, the abolition of economic, political and philanthropic discrimination is the first order of the day, not for the good of Negroes alone, but for the nation as a whole."

The word "power" historically has been a provocative one. Ancient rulers exercised absolute power. Later kings were to rule by "divine right." Under Stalin's form of communism his power was total, backed by a ruthless secret police. Even now, young Russians who write novels, poems and essays that their government finds critical are sentenced to long prison terms at hard labor.

Use of the phrase "black power" causes many persons to think only of the symbol of Stokely Carmichael, who advocates burning cities and the destruction of this country.

For perhaps a clear majority of young American Negroes (or black Americans), the phrase means something else entirely. It gets, more personally, at the larger problem discussed by Dr. Mays.

They want pride and identity—pride in being a Negro—and to identify with the genuine greatness of much of African history. Not too much is known of it. There were great cities and an attempt will be made on this matter.

All this and the psychology of this seeking for personal "power" are easily comprehended, proper and commendable.

The South's story of education is too well known to belabor. That the system and the prejudices of the past discriminated and retard us today is not denied. Chiefly neglected by the white community and philanthropy in the past were the Negro colleges.

The nation and each community can use, and be better off for, a sharing of goals and the various aspects of "power" necessary to that end.

Dr. Mays' critique of our present situation, accurate as it seems, overlooks one crucial aspect of power dynamics: Black people must create their own power. We have as a race generally overlooked the nature of power and its relation to our place in the nation's life. It is unquestionable that many black people have sought to build power—and equally unquestionable that the obstacles to their efforts have been overwhelming. But it must also be recognized that the cultural tradition of black people in the United States is stamped with the servility and dependence on white people that is the legacy of slavery. Professor David Riesman has described how Jews in the Nazi concentration camps came to accept the incidental friendly acts of their guards as acts of genuine kindness, rather than as inadequate gestures from men guilty of terrible oppression. For black people in the United States today the situation is essentially the same. Individual white men may use their power generously to provide for the basic survival needs of black people, but the prolonged acceptance of such generosity is inappropriate in a free society. For genuine freedom and justice, black people must have the power to provide for their own basic needs.

Several years ago our daughter Carolyn, then five years old, became angry that she was not allowed the freedom to walk home alone from school. I shall never forget what she said to me: "Daddy, I'm not a little girl anymore. I'm getting to be a big girl now, and you don't want me to grow up. But you had better stop oppressing me!" The message came through loud and clear. Carolyn had already recognized a truth that too many adult black people have long failed to see: Those who have power will seek to maintain and extend it, and those who want power must fight to achieve it.

Every individual possesses a latent sense of his own dignity and worth, which he can assert as a form of power. And power respects power, as can be seen in our home lives. Children wrest from their parents the power to control their own destinies, and in this way they mature. But, if a husband abuses his wife and she responds with anything less than total affirmation of her dignity and worth, then she shares the responsibility for his brutality.

The same is true on a larger scale, in society as a whole, where black men have failed to use the power implicit in their numbers to assert their worth in the face of indignities inflicted by white men. Black men have responded to white men with patience and even accommodation, but such a response is appropriate only between equals. When power is all on one side, paternalism of the most degrading kind is the result.

The racism of our society, initiated by white men but still alive only with the complicity of black men, has taught the latter to look upon themselves as less than men. And men who look upon themselves with contempt do not have the strength to win maturity and self-respect. But, as the spreading upheavals in our cities suggest, they can destroy themselves and others with them.

The vicious cycle begun by white men must be ended by appropriate power responses from black men. Yet white men have a role even now, that of catalysts. Indeed the growing recognition among some self-hating black people that too often "white makes right" is already prompting large numbers of them to shed servility and join the struggle for power.

Not long ago I appeared on a television program with Senator Vance Hartke of Indiana and several other speakers. A portion of the time was spent in discussion of the

term "black power." As I explained then, my message
about black power is a rather simple one. That black
people in general suffer from negative identity feelings
is clear from the alarming growth of social and psychi-
atric evidence of self-hatred. They must learn to accept
and appreciate themselves and their God-given—hence
glorious—blackness. And to do so, black people, who are
now powerless, need power.

The word "power" itself raises questions that are fundamental in our national life. All Americans—black and
white—must come to terms with their own identities and
with the problem of equitable power relations. My book
Black Power and Urban Unrest (1967) has been cited
for its contributions to brotherhood and human dignity.

After my television appearance, I received a letter that
takes us from where we are to where we hope to go in
this discussion. It suggests rather clearly that, if we are
to alter our present course of self-destruction, we must
redefine the tasks ahead. I am grateful to the lady who
wrote the letter for permission to reprint it:

Dear Dr. Wright,

My husband and I watched and listened to, with
great interest, the Kupcinet Show on which you appeared Saturday night (Sunday morning!).

There was much of relevance on that program, relating both to our position in Vietnam and the racial
unrest at home, and both are matters of concern to
me, but I would like to address myself to your conversation in particular because it was deeply encouraging.

I have felt for some time—specifically, since I
viewed the PBL program on police action and racial
riots—that not only is the white community just as
responsible for what goes on in its cities where there
are black ghettos as is the black community, but also

that if the white community wants to do something about the riots and general unrest, it should look to itself for the answers.

When Park Forest very recently passed its comprehensive open housing ordinance, I was made aware, by various discussions on the matter, of the sometimes patronizing attitude of the white "liberal" toward his black brother. This attitude was not dominant at all, but when it did appear, it came from those people who consider themselves—and are, in fact—conscientious citizens and humanitarians.

This led me from there to the belief that if responsible white persons want to take some kind of social action today, it should be, first of all, a contribution to or dialogue within the white community. I'm convinced that the Negro will do what is necessary for himself today and peaceably, if *his* white brother does not provoke him to violence and *especially* if his white brother will act decently and not continue to put road blocks in the Negro's way.

I think Senator Hartke missed this point when you made it, and is still fearful of the black power movement because he does not recognize the latent hostility of the white man—*not* in response to Negro violence, but *initially* in relation to the Negro. Every one of us in the white community, no matter how decently we've lived with or apart from Negroes, has enjoyed a built-in social superiority, which is finally being challenged. And surely every white person knows, even if unconsciously, the resentment which Negroes must feel, and now that it's coming out in the open, the white man who has not given it much thought before is scared to death.

Your description of black power was the most comprehensive one I had heard, and it confirmed in my mind the feeling I had come to that Negroes as a group must have their own strong sense of identity ("power") before relating to the white man on their (the Negroes') own terms.

This is a switch for me. I used to hope that gradually Negroes would be accepted, assimilated into the white community, and revered as co-members of the great society (albeit by a white standard). In fact, I wouldn't even have considered that to be anything but a Christian, brotherly expectation.

Now I view with anticipation and some relish—when I think of how the American Negro is going to change our whole society by his being in the mainstream and making himself felt in ways beyond jazz rhythms and sports heroes (I'm not suggesting that this has been his limit of contributions, but that it is all a lot of people have conceded)—the rise of "black power."

If I have doubts, it is about the white reaction to this emergence, at least at first.

I would like very much to contribute something to the white man's understanding of black power and his own position in relation to it.

What can I do?

Sincerely Yours,
Sabra Johnson
(Mrs. William F. Johnson)

In partial answer to Mrs. Johnson's question, I wrote to her that this book, already in outline form at that time, would suggest at least some starting points for white people who are anxious to contribute—and would describe some tasks that all of us, black and white, working in genuine cooperation, might undertake for ourselves and the whole nation at this urgent hour.

CHAPTER TWO

Setting the Record Straight

"THERE ARE FAR TOO MANY WHITE PEOPLE TELLING NE-groes what they need," says National Urban League executive director Whitney Young, "and far too few white people telling other white citizens to get off the Negro's back." Although the National Urban League is still unequivocally committed to integration, even Dr. Young, as his remarks suggest, insists that white people must first undertake certain tasks in their own communities.

Although the conviction that we must all work together for brotherhood is a reasonable one, it should not mislead us into the easy, self-defeating assumption that only joint activity by white and black people can lead to racial unity and peace. The means must be consistent with the ends, but, if we are to have genuine racial peace and progress—and to save our cities—then it is urgent that white people first pull themselves together. More specifically, in our present crisis there are a number of things that white people can do. Their basic task, fundamental to all the others, is to seek understanding and the spread of understanding.

Righting an Ancient Wrong

White people can help, first of all, by learning to understand the true nature of the racial problem, by penetrating to its roots. An incident from the life of Mrs. Oxley will illustrate. Each year the Oxleys pay a visit to the home of retired Episcopal Bishop Henry Wise Hobson of southern Ohio. Bishop and Mrs. Hobson are not pioneers in social change, but they are sensitive people, with remarkable vision and largeness of spirit. The four "oldsters," as might be expected, enjoy reminiscing, yet, until the Oxleys' most recent visit, certain "delicate" subjects were never discussed. This time, however, Mrs. Hobson asked Mrs. Oxley if she might pose a very personal question. Mrs. Oxley agreed. "I would like you to tell me," said Mrs. Hobson, "just what your early life was like."

In her characteristically quiet way, Mrs. Oxley unfolded the story of her upbringing in the South nearly eighty years ago. Her experience was well-nigh universal in the black community at that time, even though she herself is fair-skinned with delicate features. Her account shed painful light on the divided mind and morality that have enabled white America to circumscribe and abuse black men with impunity and, indeed, even with self-righteousness.

Mrs. Hobson listened painfully to the sad details of Mrs. Oxley's life as a black child in a white man's world. "Tell me honestly," she interrupted, "do you hate *all* white people?"

"No," replied Mrs. Oxley with a smile.

"Do you hate me?"

"No," Mrs. Oxley replied again, pleasantly.

"If I were you," Mrs. Hobson concluded remorsefully, "I think I would dislike white people."

In any consideration of what white people may contribute to ending the present racial crisis, there should first be an effort to see the basic need for what it is: not simply to help black people in their struggle but also to right an ancient and grievous wrong.

The Betrayal of a Dream

Lerone Bennett, Jr., provides perhaps the best available source for our understanding of the betrayal of the American dream of freedom for all. His *Before the Mayflower* (Revised Edition, 1964) presents a clear yet scholarly description of how the United States, conceived as "the land of the free and the home of the brave," fell prey to a systematic process of dehumanization unparalleled in the world's history. One must read Mr. Bennett's account to realize the impact of this painful aspect of the nation's history. His book belongs in every home. Reading it, one comes to understand how men in this land worked in the early years toward the fulfillment of a dream of freedom and equality. One can understand, and still mourn, the unfortunate circumstances that impelled a youthful and uncertain nation to compromise its humanitarian principles and betray its vision for the sake of immediate economic gain. The tragic effects of this aberration are still with us.

Mr. Bennett's book should go far toward convincing Americans that only a long-range view of personal and national self-interest provides a worthy basis for commitment, the hallmark, of course, of those who have achieved maturity and wisdom.

Our history has made us what we are, and we can achieve understanding of what we are only if we know our history. Had it not been for a particular series of events during the early years of this country's development, black people might have been integrated into the social system, as they were in Puerto Rico and Brazil, where most of the populations have dark skins. How did this difference come about?

Most of the early settlers, Europeans, as well as black men from Africa, were brought to America as indentured servants. Those white indentured servants who arrived before 1660 mixed with black indentured servants, and both black and white servants were able to earn their freedom. Of that period, Mr. Bennett has written:

> In Virginia, then, as in other colonies, the first Negro settlers fell into a well-established socio-economic groove which carried with it no implications of racial inferiority. That came later. But in the interim, a period of forty years or more, the first Negroes accumulated land, voted, testified in court and mingled with whites on a basis of equality. They owned other Negro servants. And at least one Negro imported and paid for a white servant whom he held in servitude. Negro and white servants, [historian] Kenneth Stampp says, "seemed to be remarkably unconcerned about their visible differences. They toiled together in the fields, fraternized during leisure hours, and, in and out of wedlock, collaborated in siring a numerous progeny."

So Mr. Bennett describes the racial situation at the beginning of our nation. But vast resources of cheap labor had become so necessary to the booming American economy—to southern plantations and northern finance—by the mid-seventeenth century that a new system to ensure continued easy profits had to be adopted: slavery. There were many problems in such a course, including the moral reconciliation of the prostitution of human life with the idealistic value system of the new land, but greedy men preferred not to face such unsettling questions.

The practical problems of maintaining slavery were, however, attacked with a will. For example, escaped white workers could not be identified by their color, but enslavement of blacks, who could be quickly apprehended if they escaped, solved that difficulty. Another problem was how legally to deny inheritance of plantation and other property to the children of the owners and slave women. The myth of racial inferiority was the answer, and it ultimately provided the broader justification for the inhuman exploitation of black people. Knowledge of these events is essential to an understanding of how our past has conditioned the present crisis, but they are not reported in most histories of early North America. The shame they represent makes it easy to understand why. Nonetheless, the influence of the past must be understood if we are ever to realize the early precious dream of a free United States.

The Penalties for Being Black

Beginning with Virginia in 1661, all southern states passed laws, not only committing all black people to permanent slavery, but also classifying them as chattels, the ultimate act of dehumanization. In 1663 the Maryland assembly passed a measure forbidding racial intermarriage. Part of the law read: "Divers freeborn English women, forgetful of their free condition . . . did intermarry with slaves. Such women are to be slaves of their husbands' masters." Some people believe that this law, and the acceptance of its spirit elsewhere in the nation, doomed any possibility for assimilation of black people into the white American culture. Joining with black men meant sharing whatever penalties were imposed upon black men. Degraded status and continual indignities were the fate of all who entered interracial alliances.

In 1667 Virginia ruled that Christian baptism could not confer freedom on Negroes. Maryland passed a similar law in 1671, New York in 1706, and other states thereafter. Finally, "Negro" came to be defined as "any person with some Negro ancestry," and therefore all offspring of unions between black and white have been regarded as Negroes—as black people.

Considering the penalties and restrictions applied to those who are black, there is small wonder that open social intercourse between white and black people has been drastically curtailed. The great irony is that perhaps the majority of Americans whose roots in this country extend back more than a hundred years should, by the old definition, be classified as black, so widespread have been the covert relations between the races.

Few white people in the South and Midwest are entirely without some black or Indian ancestry, and many will freely admit it. I traveled recently with a white businessman who came from a distinguished southern family. He told of how, during his youth, every deacon and trustee in his local church had sired children through black concubinage—a common practice in days before modern contraception. Sexual use of black women helped to lessen the burden and preserve the purity of white womanhood and thus became a "Christian" practice. The fair-skinned offspring of such unions were usually shipped off to relatives or schools in other places, with the result that countless numbers disappeared into the white landscape, and through their progeny, have helped to disseminate black genes among the "white" population.

Wherever groups of people live side by side, our social scientists explain, intergroup sexual relations inevitably occur, for natural appetites tend to triumph over artificial barriers. Racial relations by night are thus different from those by day. They persistently shape the "racial" character of our society, while subverting our professed morality and exposing our national hypocrisy.

"My Niggers"

A dozen or so years ago I met Judge Ormond Scott, who had been appointed by President Franklin Roosevelt to a judgeship in the District of Columbia and was highly respected in the capital.

The occasion of our meeting was a regional Alpha Phi Alpha fraternity conclave. When we were introduced, Judge Scott, dispensing with the conventional courtesies, immediately began to berate me for my part in securing the appointment to a high position in the Boston area of a man whom he considered an Uncle Tom. I immediately calmed the judge by assuring him that, had the man in question not received the job, very likely a white man, who would be totally unmindful of black people's needs, would have secured it. We agreed that perhaps it was better that at least a little color had been added to the scene.

The judge then remarked that he had wanted to meet me for some time, as I had married into a family with which he had been closely associated for many years. Judge Scott had grown up in Wilmington, North Carolina, with my wife's grandfather John Taylor and his brother Robert, who were black sons of one of the white patricians of that city. Near the turn of the century there was a riot against the local black people, and young Scott had to leave town for his safety. He told me how the Taylor brothers had been protected by their patron. Word had been passed to the white community by the elder Taylor: "Leave my niggers alone!"

These two fair-skinned—but not too fair-skinned—off-

spring of the southern aristocracy were well taken care
of. John was sent to Harvard University and Robert to
the Massachusetts Institute of Technology. John Taylor
served for some time as an official in the local customs
office. Robert Taylor served as chief engineer and vice-
principal of Booker T. Washington's Tuskegee Institute.
He subsequently served as vice-president of Tuskegee
for a number of years and died there in 1944 after being
stricken in the chapel that he had built.

The Taylors are representative of the black bourgeoisie,
or middle class, which has been much maligned and much
misunderstood by both black and white people. They have
been looked upon as the favored few, with emphasis on
few. White America points to the Taylors and the Oxleys
as evidence that relations between white and black Americans are not really so bad. After all, the Taylors and the
Oxleys have achieved reasonable success, haven't they?
Yet these successful so-called middle-class black people
know that they are among the most compromised black
people in America.

They know that, although they have not received the
legal inheritances and status due them, they have suffered
far less indignity than have the masses of black people.
They also know that they have obeyed the rules of white
America but have still been dealt with by whites as "black
men" rather than simply as men. Fisk and Howard Universities were founded for them. A young member of the
Harper family, an eminent black family descended from
General Robert E. Lee, tells of mentioning to a group of
New England liberals that she had attended Fisk University. "That's our missionary school!" was the devastating response. "We are all so very proud of what we do
to help uplift your kind!"

The old-line black bourgeoisie is largely unknown to
white America. For most of a century its members have
kept themselves hidden from white people as much as

possible. They have been taught to avoid white people studiously, for in the prevailing order every contact with white people involves some measure of threat and uncertainty. Large numbers of white people therefore see only black menial workers, for the bourgeois-type do not ride public transportation and traditionally keep their women very close to home.

I shall never forget my surprise when one of the Taylors told me that she would not eat with white people except on rare occasions associated with her husband's work. As I was at the time a doctrinaire integrationist, I was puzzled and even outraged—until I heard the explanation. Since emancipation members of the black middle class have been sought out by white people for token friendship. Many have accepted such friendship. Most, however, have come to realize that accepting friendship from white people is like purchasing stock in guaranteed frustration. Considering the penalties for consorting with black people as presently defined by society, it is almost inevitable that white people will welsh on the friendship when their children reach the age of sexual awareness. Black people, expecting eventual rejection, reason that "an ounce of prevention is worth a pound of cure."

One may well ask what such an attitude accomplishes. For black people the answer is obviously survival and sanity. White people must understand the dynamics of their own unconscious, culturally conditioned behavior if we are all to move nearer to where we would like to be. It is obvious that white liberals teaching in black schools, white missionaries among black people, and even white clergymen with mixed middle-class congregations do not want their children to marry black people. The dividing line is still there, whether we like it or not. The too rare exceptions to this statement serve only to highlight its general truth.

If I were a white man today, I doubt that I would want

my son or daughter to marry a black person, for what man wants his child to join a group that possesses insufficient self-respect and insubstantial control over its own destiny? When black people begin to address themselves more effectively to the issues of status and power, then perhaps we shall cease talking of "intermarriage" and shall speak instead of "marriage."

The success of the few like the elder Taylor's "niggers," tends to obscure the over-all failure of black people to enter the mainstream of American social life. Like Adam Clayton Powell they occupy precarious positions in business or government only at the pleasure or whim of white people, and they know it. The altogether arbitrary, though legal, treatment of the Powells—and the growing desperation of black people as a whole, whose low status and relative powerlessness the black middle class certainly shares —serve to remind them that, whatever the outward appearances, all black men belong to one class, indelibly set apart by the color black.

That descendants of the so-called "house Negroes" are now becoming militant is a source of surprise and consternation to many white people. A recent study at Brandeis University revealed that the black middle class type represents major spawning ground for the growing militance among black people. But white people should understand their own part in creating this militance.

White Benevolence

"Haven't we been good to you?" is the question that well-intentioned white liberals often ask. "Why are you now rejecting us?"

The obvious reason is that, before the help recently given by white liberals in the so-called "freedom movement," black people had not even the choice of rejecting the ostensibly helping hand of white people.

The March on Washington in 1963 can be regarded on one hand as a fizzle and on the other as a formidable prod to progress. Its immediate results included more legislation and the completion of at least one phase of the freedom movement itself. But the intense enthusiasm generated by the movement precluded critical assessment of the worsening plight of black Americans, and inevitably some disillusionment followed.

In their quest for freedom, black men began to question the effectiveness of the supposed assistance of those in power. For example, in 1965 major national resources were mustered to pass the Voting Rights Bill; yet, at the same time, it has been estimated that urban renewal, with its vast dislocations of black people, was in effect disfranchising more black people than the Voting Rights Bill would add to the voting rolls in thirty years. Who decided for *us* that we needed a voting rights bill? Who gave *leadership* in affairs relating to our lives? Some black men concluded that white people, who represent the culture in power, should no longer define the goals or provide the leadership for black people in their quest for power.

Although in this quest, some help from those already in power may be needed, white definition of our problems clearly must be rejected. The white liberal, whose protective attitude has always implied that he "knows what is best," views this new attitude as rejection, insult, effrontery. Not long ago I attended, with the Reverend Quinland Gordon of the Executive Council of the Episcopal Church, a meeting of white executives of social agencies. They had gathered to discuss what they might do to assist black people's new quest for identity, status, and control over their own destiny. The meeting largely failed, except that perhaps for the first time these white

liberals involved in black affairs began to see some of the
negative effects of their own cultural conditioning.

When Father Gordon, who was the only other black
man present, tried earnestly to emphasize the difference
between assistance on one hand and leadership on the
other, one white leader burst into a tirade:

> All I can hear is that you black folks are rejecting
> us. You're saying to us "Get out!" You want every-
> thing we've got, and we had better hand it over. If
> you can't have everything we've got, you're going to
> tear things apart. If it's a choice between your killing
> us or my killing you, I'm certain about my own per-
> sonal choice. I feel like getting into my car, driving
> home and getting my shotgun, and killing you and
> all your kind. You folks are asking for a race war.
> You're in the minority, and, by George, we're going
> to all get ready to get you first.

The great tragedy revealed here is not so much the
progressive illogic of one angry man as the certainty that
countless white people throughout the country are caught
in the same type of thinking. We shall have more to say
in Chapter 8 about this tragedy and its awesome national
implications.

The sometimes distracted and negative reactions of
white liberals are clearly understandable, however. Parents teach their children to stand on their own. Yet, when
the children show signs of doing so, the parents admonish
them for being "uppity" or disrespectful, for the change is
highly unsettling. It would clearly be unrealistic to expect those who have guided black people for 300 years,
without expecting them to grow to independence at all,
to be other than disoriented by the recent efforts of black
people to stand on their own. But black people, to say the
least, cannot afford unnecessary enemies. As we shall see
in another chapter, black people must understand their

own behavior and take the initiative in interpreting it to the white men whose cooperation they must seek.

Without the recent freedom movement (a mixed blessing, like most blessings), black people would not be at the point of creative rebellion today. The freedom movement both shaped and was shaped by Malcolm X. It provided him with a platform for much of his critical and creative work. The radical alternatives he posed, on the other hand, by creating anxiety among white people, increased the opportunities for the more conservative leaders of the N.A.A.C.P. and the Urban League—and Dr. Martin Luther King—to be heard and heeded. The following story, possibly apocryphal, is told about one of Dr. King's campaigns in a southern town. His efforts had been unavailing. On the morning that he was planning to leave in utter defeat, the newspapers carried the headline "Malcolm X Comes to Town." The insistent ringing of his telephone awakened Dr. King. "Martin, Martin," the excited voice explained, "this is the mayor. Just what was it that you have been trying to say?"

All who have worked in the movement for freedom have reinforced one another's efforts, even though often in mutually vexing ways. That new situations teach new duties, however, should be abundantly clear. The Ku Klux Klan ran my family out of Shreveport, Louisiana, when my twin brother and I were six months old, yet I am deeply grateful. If it had not been for the Klan, we would not be where we are today!

Dr. H. C. Hudson of Los Angeles, my sister Lydia's godfather, was compelled to leave Shreveport at the same time as my family and that of a Dr. Liddell. My father, Dr. Hudson, and Dr. Liddell had, during the heyday of the Klan, regularly risked their lives to help sharecroppers learn to read, write, and keep records of their credit accounts with the local merchants. The reading and writing were tolerated by the local white citizenry, but the record keeping upset the established order. Threats and actual bodily harm came to the three men. My father was beaten and left for dead.

Those who know Dr. Hudson know that there is no bitterness in him or in his compatriots. He serves today on the national board of the N.A.A.C.P. He explained to me recently that he is often regarded as one who does not understand the aspirations of the younger generation. "Actually, I want always to keep up with the times," he said. Now nearly eighty years old, he is a distinguished and still useful public servant. Our elder statesmen should know that they must keep up with the times and train the leadership that will shape the future. The past cannot be allowed to impose upon the present. But black men must honor the spirit of those who, under painful and bitter oppression, paved the way for us. One who cannot accept his past cannot accept himself. We must use the past as a stepping stone to the future. We must honor the good with which the past has invested the present and then move on to newer and better things.

White people must also understand the past. Their noble but blighted dreams may be recaptured if they can learn the lessons of past ugliness and move on as wiser men toward greater good for all.

CHAPTER THREE

The Need for
Helping Hands

ONCE A NEW UNDERSTANDING OF OUR RACIAL PROBLEM IS
achieved, white people can best serve the nation's most
critical internal needs by acting not as leaders but as facili-
tators of efforts by black people to obtain power.

The definition of "facilitate" in *Webster's Handy College Dictionary* is "to make easier." The same dictionary
defines "easy" as "1. not difficult; 2. comfortable; tranquil;
3. not oppressive." These qualities are precisely those that
white people should seek to achieve in their relations with
black people. Without a doubt, white America has so far
made things difficult, uncomfortable, and oppressive for
black people. The result has been—as mounting urban
dislocations attest—lack of tranquillity in the nation.

Just what is involved in facilitating black people's efforts to develop both for their own good and the greater
enrichment of the nation? Several specific suggestions
can be made; a spirit of acceptance should lead to continual discovery of further things that white people can
contribute.

39

Junior Partners

First, white people must learn to relinquish the role of
patron, however appropriate it seemed in the past, for
that of junior partner in the black people's struggle for
power. Patrons can dictate. Partners must both speak and
listen. One of the greatest offenses that well-meaning
white people have long committed against thoughtful
black people has been to press upon them unsought advice
—and without doubt heeding it has often served to ensure
black survival. But, to a person who knows that he is not
a child, a ward, or a client, any further "talking to" from
the self-appointed patron is unwelcome. It does not facilitate; it is in fact oppressive.

What is the alternative for white people? The answer
can be given in one word: "ask." Ask *black people* how
you may be of help. Then your ideas, conceived within
the framework of *their* expressed needs and aspirations,
may find a welcome.

As I have already pointed out, partners must both speak
and listen. Still, as in many fields of endeavor, in black
people's striving, the partnership calls for senior and junior
members. It is the new role of junior partner that white
people must now learn quickly for the tranquillity of the
nation. In Chapters 9 and 10 we shall examine these tasks
that may most profitably be undertaken by equal partners.
A junior partner knows that the senior partner sets the
agenda and exercises greater control and responsibility. A
junior partner thus primarily listens, then acts on the advice of the senior partner.

I find T. George Harris, a former editor of *Look*, the
ideal junior partner. George telephones me at the oddest
times, sometimes three or four times a week. "I'm troubled," he will say. "Just now I heard the news that something new was going to break for the benefit of black

people. When I checked the story out, I found out that it was planned *for* black people *by* a bunch of white folks who couldn't care less for black folks. But, by damn it, on the surface it sounds good!"

George Harris is a self-styled "Kentucky cracker." Although he is a former Rhodes scholar and has a record of many notable journalistic achievements, he believes that the key to his creative insight lies in the marginal circumstances of his early upbringing. "I get madder than a wet hen," he often says, "whenever I see a black man trying to get over or ignore his black experience and try to be altogether white. In the first place, it's impossible. In the second place, he's cheating the hell out of himself and other people. It's in the keeping of my experience as a Kentucky cracker that I am enabled to see and understand many things that my well-bred WASP-ish compatriots can't see and understand. You black folks had better learn to keep your old experience and simply add the new!"

George uses me. He tests ideas on me and shares new information and insights. But, whenever he ventures a conclusion, I think that he is usually wrong. He appreciates the frankness of my reactions. "I wish white folks, who represent power," he says, "would learn that they need to share their data with black people, and then listen. Those with power just can't decide on the needs of those who don't have power. It's this way with parents and kids. Black people had better devise some means of doing all the basic planning for their own needs. The rest of us can at best simply help you."

George has been after me for nearly two years to help him initiate a new form of dialogue between black and white people, one in which white people will supply the data and black people will supply the answers. A major gripe of his is that too many people want to *do* things but that all too few want to take the time to discover what really needs to be done. He is convinced that reliance on

the old clichés will lead us headlong into disaster. Thinking and acting, he cries, must occur simultaneously. To
attempt one without the other, he believes, is playing a
fool's game.

In every community in the nation, white people should
be listening to black people. Either white or black people
may take the initiative in getting together. One word, of
warning, however: Those who do not respect their peers
in other groups actually reflect contempt for the other
groups. Highly trained white people must meet as equals
with highly trained black people.

So many of our government, church, and social-agency
programs make the mistake of expecting the least trained
and technically competent black people to relate freely to
white men with the highest training and financial resources. When a poor black man and woman scrimp and
save to provide higher education for their children so that
they can learn to understand, articulate, interpret, and
prescribe for the needs of their community, the children
may decide to live in different communities, but they
understand and care about their parents' needs. Yet, when
government antipoverty and model-cities programs seek
"maximum feasible participation" of "local residents," of
"the poor," the trained leadership of the sons and daugh-
ters of the "local residents" and "the poor" is excluded.
When the trained and powerful try to assist the untrained
and powerless, even though the "consent" of the latter is
given, there can be no genuine relationship.

The trained whites must deal instead with their black
peers. And the latter, with their more direct interest in the
problems of all black people, must direct the effort. Those
whites who wish to facilitate it must learn to *assist* in re-
lieving oppression and in making the struggle of the oppressed easier.

In the New Testament, there is a saying that white
people in particular should take to heart in our racial crisis

today: "He who would be chief among you, let him be servant of all." (Luke 22:26.) Black people need—and the nation's peace and safety require—the service of those whose past posture has been one of lordliness. White people who are willing to serve as thoughtful junior partners to thoughtful black people will contribute much to the nation in these perilous times. Will you volunteer?

"No Stepping Aside"

Will Clarkson of the Westminster Community House in Buffalo recently said to me: "I am determined to be of help with those in the black community with whom I have been working. The present difficulties and uncertainties are not going to cause me to leave my responsibilities. I know that I must alter my relationships. But I am not going to leave my work. I want to serve as best I can. How do you feel that this can be done?"

Will Clarkson is a dedicated, highly responsible, and open-minded man. May his tribe increase. White people are more than ever needed in tasks relating to the immediate interests of the black community. We need white people like the Will Clarksons who have the courage to ask how they can best help.

My immediate answer to Mr. Clarkson was that we could work out an answer together. We subsequently agreed that we should spend an evening together discussing the matter, which we did several weeks later. A simple but basic mistake that so many black brothers make is to offer serious or substantial answers to questions that have been raised on the spur of the moment. Any question should at least be checked out for seriousness. Then it should be dealt with—not lightly, but in the most thoughtful and substantial way. Instead of pat answers the questioner should be given responses that will turn his thinking into new channels that will enable him to work out his own answers in the future. We shall have offered little serious help if others must repeatedly turn to us for next steps each time they want to take a further step in what should be a continuous, self-sustaining process. One of the best ways to respond is to plant seed ideas and then to elicit answers, if possible, from the questioner himself.

Many times professional consultation is necessary in planning and carrying out effective programs to help black people. Despite my emphasis on the necessity for involving trained black people, a caveat is in order: I do not intend to go to the extreme and claim that blackness guarantees omniscience. When competent advice is necessary, competent advice should be obtained, from whatever source makes it available. Not long ago, a group of black people in one community was bemoaning the fact that more than 95 percent of the consultation budget for the local antipoverty program was going to white experts on black affairs. My obvious amusement was a source of annoyance. I asked, "Just why should antipoverty consultative funds go to black people when practically any black man, whom antipoverty officials might ask for advice on any matter whatsoever, will be more than glad to give free and presumably competent technical advice?" The question reflects far more truth than may at first be apparent. One cause of our failure to plan thoughtfully for black needs lies in the need of so many black people to feel that they are "somebody." The white world has demeaned black men in such a way that many black men will grasp at any straw to appear worthwhile. This white-induced black pathology effectively works to the detriment of the nation's peace.

One thing is certain: People do not eagerly commit themselves to any cause on the basis of pat answers to serious questions. They must share in a process of discovery. Whenever white people today seek serious answers, they should consider the possibility of paying competent black advisers, perhaps on a permanent basis, to lay the groundwork for turning over to these advisers total control of the continuing effort—in fact they could treat their own role as that of pump primer.

Will Clarkson has been chairman of the board of directors of a largely black community center. He is aware of two things: first that black people need images of black leadership and black success at every level and, second, that black people must have control—and awareness of control—over all matters relating intimately to their own destiny. For these reasons, Will Clarkson will resign as board chairman.

The servant role can be a creative role, however. Only in this way may urban peace and national survival be assured. Simple, thoughtful humility on the part of white people at this dangerous point in the nation's life would do more perhaps than anything else to ensure tranquillity. I often give to white people a simple "cultural-deprivation test," the object of which is to demonstrate that all people are deprived in terms of the cultures with which they happen to be unfamiliar. It is a humorous test, and its humor affords the opportunity of pointing out to white people their tragic unwillingness to ask advice or to seek help from black people when they themselves obviously do not know the answers to some of the questions presented to them.

The test consists of three spelling questions presented in exaggerated southern dialect. Almost any group of words will do. I frequently use, with a very long drawl, the southern pronunciation of "right," "here," and "I don't know." When the test is given in a group, most often in the humor of guessing the correct spelling of the words at least one white person will laugh at what would otherwise be a very painful act of self-discovery. "Guess what I noticed that we have been doing?" is the characteristic opener. "Ordinarily, we would *ask* to have the words used in a sentence. But we as white people just aren't in the habit of asking black people for advice."

Humility may be difficult to accept, but it is worth making the effort, in order to cope more effectively with the pressing problems of our communities. The nation as a whole—and each of its communities—could save itself much internal pain if only there were a willingness to listen and heed the helpful words of those black people whose training and experience can help the nation most. Dr. Kenneth Clark once exclaimed that professionally trained black people, whose fortunes and loyalties coincide in many ways with those of white people, are among the most misused in the nation. Their voices, loyal even in opposition, must somehow be heard by white men. It must be recognized quite clearly that permanent white attention depends largely upon black status and power, but the immediate safety of the nation depends upon white people's heeding the sane advice of black people *now*. Whether or not black people as a whole succeed in building the power to be heard in this nation, discerning white people must at least see to it that sane and sensitive black men help to shape the present course of our corporate life in crucial areas.

The Proper Pegs

Putting the proper pegs in the proper holes is a game that has been played for many centuries and in many cultures. Children learn that square pegs do not fit round holes and the reverse. Yet, in facing so many of our urban problems, we continue to match the wrong resources to the problems.

Not long ago a chief of police in New York's Westchester County was asked what he thought of a decision by

Governor Nelson Rockefeller to use state troopers for a crackdown on the narcotics racket in Harlem. The police chief applauded the governor's concern but questioned the use of wholesome-looking white men as undercover agents in a black community. Presumably narcotics traffic *is* a problem for state law enforcement, but, if we seriously intend to do the job, we must use the specific kind of law-enforcement officers who can actually do it. Otherwise, the whole attempt is an exercise in futility.

In quelling or containing civil disorders, the mere presence of uniformed white policemen has far too often contributed to lawlessness. They are not the *best* resource for containing black rebellion. The Presidential Commission on Civil Disorders indicated that, ideally, men sympathetic to the black community should participate in dealings with it at such times. In every major community in the nation, unarmed black men—and women—could and should be recruited, deputized, and trained as officers of *peace*. Many of our presently unemployed black youth and adult black males could and should be used for this purpose. If our intention is to have *peace* and *order,* then the most appropriate available resources should be used for this purpose.

It is a sad fact of our society that we so greatly compromise our officers of the peace. We do not define their role in terms appropriate to our times, nor do we provide the sophisticated training and commensurate pay necessary for adequate peace keeping. Postgraduate education should be required of our full-time officers of the peace, and a completely new orientation toward promoting peace should become standard. Officers of the peace should constitute a great profession, distinguished by the highest intelligence, sophistication, and training. Our police forces —along with every enterprise serving the public—should employ black people in equitable proportions at every level. In my earlier book, *Ready to Riot* (1968), I dealt with other problems of professionalizing the police and with matters calling for intimate knowledge and understanding by the police. In my forthcoming *Programs for Power: New Approaches to Urban Regeneration,* a model police-academy curriculum and an outline of the major task for officers of the peace, suited to both our present and future needs, will be presented. It should suffice here to say that the best resources should be used to accomplish any purpose. The police in our cities should be the best. The best assistance for peaceable and unarmed control or containment of civil disorders should and can be secured from local citizens. It should be borne in mind that deaths during the rebellions result almost entirely from white men's, not black men's, bullets.

The application of the best resources to accomplish immediate tasks should be the central concern in our urban school systems and in our social-work and urban-planning agencies as well. Dr. James Paul Comer, a distinguished past director of the Yale Child Development Center who is presently working at the National Institute of Mental Health, has emphasized the crucial importance of black leadership in all largely black-related concerns. He points out that, although capable white leadership may offer the intellectual assurance of possible success for black people, the emotive message—"I did; therefore, you can"—can be transmitted only by successful black men and women.

The misuse—insufficient use—of employed black men and women is a major cause of black apathy toward learning job skills. If one studies hard and still gets nowhere fast, black people reason, why apply oneself at all? The fact that a white high school dropout may still in 1968 earn more than can a black man with two years of college training is a serious indictment of white America.

Job-training programs are an effective, although not necessarily a deliberate, way to keep black men from finding suitable employment. The jobs that call for little or no training, even in our cities, are held chiefly by white people. All black men are qualified to work—as they are —in *some* capacity. In wartime we demonstrated that all men can be fitted to useful jobs when the situation demands. What black men need is less job training than skin grafting. If our unemployed black men were white, most of them would be employed.

Every white businessman in the United States will find it worthwhile to read Dr. Comer's lead article in the April 1967 issue of *Scientific American;* it is entitled "The Social Force of the Negro." White businessmen who are interested in providing job opportunities for black men should start integrating at the top. Simple justice demands no less. When white business seeks to recruit black men at the bottom without visibly affording room at the top for those already employed, it is like inviting investors in good times to put money in limited-dividend stocks. Most firms striving honestly for equitable employment practices should retain capable long- or short-term black consultants. Otherwise they are responsible for placing criminal burdens on the social welfare and for prolonging the underlying causes of disturbances to the public peace.

It should be clear that the capabilities and experience of black men and women, who have shared in black community life, are the primary resource in planning for specifically black community needs, yet a resource that is criminally unused or misused. Our total national commitment—and that of each local community—is to the most efficient orderly progress; and our collective aim must therefore be the immediate and massive correction of this serious deficiency in the use of our resources.

Our so-called "antipoverty" efforts—which are ostensibly designed to ease or eradicate black poverty—actually have worked to widen the economic gap between white and black Americans. It is notorious that most of the funds allocated for professional help to meet black needs

—for "urban planning"—go to white institutions and
white people. Cities consist of people, and solutions to
urban problems mean planning for needs symbolized most
clearly by black people who represent urban problems *in
extremis*. Small wonder that the more planning there is for
so-called "urban needs," the worse things have come to be!

The N.A.A.C.P., the National Urban League, the Southern Christian Leadership Conference, the Congress of
Racial Equality, the Student Non-Violent Coordinating
Committee, the National Council of Negro Women, the
National Association of Marketing Developers, the National Medical and National Dental Associations, and
other black fraternal, educational, religious, civic, and
business groups—despite their obvious willingness, commitment, and painfully won wisdom—must still beg for
their meager funds while white men and white institutions are continually receiving vast amounts to plan and
execute visionary and abortive programs for black people.

Both because of the understanding necessary to deal
constructively and fruitfully with urban needs and because of the worsening economic plight of black people,
it should be obvious that no white people—with only the
most extraordinary exceptions—should profit from planning for largely black community needs. There are more
than enough presently unused planning skills in any established and reputable black community group that can be
put to work for the public good. The same hands that
have generally engineered black survival now can and
must be used to reverse our misdirected and foolhardy
rush toward national disaster.

Furthermore, in order for black people to have equity
in the nation they must be granted—as veterans are—the
benefit of a "handicap." Rudimentary justice decrees that
black people be treated in such a manner as deliberately
and speedily to close the economic gap that was created

to their detriment—and according to a firm time schedule with clear accountability for failures.

Malcolm Talbot, vice-president of the Newark campus of Rutgers University and formerly Associate Dean of the Rutgers Law School, repeatedly emphasizes that white America must treat black America according to accepted legal principles of equity and restitution. Black men, denied or only partly granted opportunities in the past, must, according to the principles developed throughout our legal history, be given preference in every enterprise in the nation. This restitution is a *sine qua non* for every black community, and anything less will compound our already far too serious problems.

The use of black people in the planning and control of their own community needs must be recognized as elementary justice and only a beginning at that. White America—as the clear result of injustice in white and black power relations—exercises control of most resources for our black communities. For the peace, efficient progress, and fulfillment of the nation, competent black men and women—from the "old-line" organizations and from the new—must control these resources for themselves.

To heed the ceaseless cry of black men for freedom from bondage and exploitation is immediately possible for each local and national agency or executive that exercises control over the destinies of black people. The spirit that seeks for each man the simple mastery of his own house and for each community, however it is defined, control of its own destiny, is the spirit of liberty, the only valid one in the founding and development of our nation.

The continued control of black men's destinies by white men must be recognized as an unconscionable extension of a dehumanizing system. The growing symptoms of unrest in our cities signify that this system has failed to generate from within itself independent efforts toward self-sufficiency and self-respect. Instead, black men increasingly proclaim their revulsion and indignation. Self-respecting white men would assuredly do no less. Indeed, it is postponement of demands to "cease and desist" that have intensified our present predicament. White men and women who want peace, progress, and the efficiency that alone brings prosperity must—even at this late and urgent hour—do all within their power to eliminate quickly the basic control by whites of black people.

The cry of Moses before the Egyptian pharaoh, so Senator Edward Brooke has reminded us, rises again from every black community in the land, calling to white brothers who still control and, consciously or unconsciously, exploit black men: "Let my people go!"

If continued reliance mainly on white professionals in black community planning could provide the needed freedom—and awareness of freedom—and could close the perilous economic gap between black and white Americans, then our present policies would have to continue. But, as it cannot, then all our governmental, social-agency, and civic planning for largely black community needs should be reviewed with equity, contributions to self-development, and efficiency as the criteria for new and more constructive approaches.

Our state and Federal governments must provide both fresh resources and continuing guarantees that our society functions for the greatest good for all. But, first and last, the good sense and self-interest of our private citizens should ensure that the most efficient and just means are always applied to serve the common good. If they cannot, we as a nation shall have definitely failed to fulfill the dream of justice and the good life for all.

CHAPTER FOUR

Making
Educational Changes

"BY ALL KNOWN CRITERIA, THE MAJORITY OF URBAN AND
rural slum schools are failures." Such was the conclusion
of the recent Presidential Panel on Educational Research
and Development. The same judgment might be made of
many institutions in our society.

Any element of a society that survives long enough to
evolve into an institution does so by its ability to satisfy
certain needs of the society or by its compatibility with
the established pattern of social relationships. In turn
those who control these institutions have an interest in
preserving order and stability in the society as a whole. It
is important to understand this point because it is often
lightly assumed that our schools and churches—along
with our other social institutions—are natural agencies of
social change. They are not. They are designed to uphold
the existing order. Only when this point is acknowledged
may we begin to understand the mounting failure of all
our institutions to keep pace with the needs of our rapidly
changing society.

For the several generations that will follow us, the only
certainty that we can forecast is the certainty of change

itself. Redefinition of both "order" and of "institutional" life must be quickly achieved. Otherwise, our schools, our churches, and our government, business, and civic agencies will continue, with perhaps the best intentions and the greatest zeal, on their present headlong course toward disaster.

In this light, we may recognize the pathos of demands for order by a former Vice-President of the United States as he righteously campaigns for higher office. Richard Nixon's logic is reasonable and correct only if viewed in the light of outworn conceptions of the public good; but reliance on such conceptions now can only subvert the very safety of the nation. If he could accept newer social-scientific and philosophical ideas—the extension and application of which our society so desperately needs—a man of Mr. Nixon's integrity, experience, and seriousness might be among the most capable leaders that our nation could expect to find in the days ahead. His needs, the satisfaction of which he would welcome, are but symptomatic of the needs of our society as a whole.

Our Public Schools

The public schools, particularly in our cities, are failing to develop the nation's human potential precisely because such development requires openness to basic social change. A number of classic studies have demonstrated clearly that education gears its production of graduates —both in numbers and in caliber at each grade level of exit—to anticipated local or national economic needs.

The opposite, and socially more desirable, course for the schools would be to use all reasonable means to discover and develop the potential of each student. Then our social and economic order could be shaped and adapted to the unfolding needs and gifts of our population.

At present, our inner-city schools have a national drop-out rate of more than 50 per cent; fewer than 5 per cent of inner-city high-school graduates proceed to any form of higher education. The Presidential Panel on Educational Research and Development noted the alarming fact that most young people who leave our inner-city schools are "ill-prepared to lead a satisfying, useful life or to participate successfully in the community." Clearly more than minor surgery is required. Major redirection of the entire system of inner-city schools must be achieved if a national catastrophe is to be averted.

Sylvia Porter, in a syndicated column significantly headed "Education Is Fuel for Economic Fires" (February 28, 1968), spells out this same sad story as described by a white educator (the italics are mine):

By 1975, only seven years away, the U.S. Labor Department predicts nearly one in three young workers beginning their careers in the United States will have had at least some college education vs. a little more than one in four today. By 1975, only 29 per cent will have had less than a high school education vs. 36 per cent today.

In this period, the most rapid growth in jobs will be in fields demanding the most education. Jobs in the professional occupations will increase at least twice as fast as the overall number of jobs in all fields. By contrast, jobs for operatives and craftsmen will increase relatively slowly, and jobs for low skilled or unskilled laborers actually are expected to decrease.

Yet, the frightening fact is that there are 3,000,000 high school dropouts in the 16-21 year age bracket in the U.S. today. These are the youngsters whose unemployment rates are nearly double those for graduates (and, if a Negro dropout, as high as 19 per cent).

Clearly, a crucial need is for more and better teachers trained to work with minority and disadvantaged youngsters, particularly in big city slums and in remote rural areas. In many cases and in many places a complete overhaul of the college-oriented high school curriculum will be the only answer. Drastic upgrading and updating of vocational courses will be essential, if we are to persuade potential dropouts to stay in school and if we are to equip them for the actual jobs in which they will be able to find employment.

Again, clearly we must provide far more motivation than we are already providing to encourage every bright, talented young American to climb as far up the educational ladder, to college and beyond, as he possibly can.

Unless we do all of these things, or at least unless we do them better than we are now doing, we will be failing to keep the American promise and we also will be seriously retarding the nation's overall economic growth in this era.

In short, at stake is actually the very growth of our nation. Education is and will be ever more the fuel for economic expansion.

We must remember that the "dropouts" of which Miss Porter speaks are human beings—people. Any society that claims "success" while any of its members lacks opportunity to develop his own life to the fullest is less than humanely inspired. We must come to see total human development as a moral imperative. Not one human life can our nation afford to waste; not one potential contributor to the good of all can it afford to sacrifice.

How can white people best help to overcome the educational catastrophe that our inner-city schools represent in terms of lost, wasted black human potential that must be used for the fulfillment of the nation's promise?

Face Up to White Racism

The reports of the several local and national commissions on civil disorders have placed the blame for "nonlearning" upon those who share immediate responsibility for the schools. The New Jersey Governor's Select Commission on Civil Disorders recommended that the state take over the Newark public schools. Rampant racism in every enterprise in the nation's life was cited by the Presidential Commission on Civil Disorders as the prime source of mounting unrest. For those who operate our schools to persist in their refusal to accept, even to recognize, their own culturally conditioned racism as a potential "Achilles' heel" may prove more disastrous for the nation than any other single factor over which local government authorities exercise control.

All who are brought up in the United States, or in any society, are shaped both spontaneously and deliberately by its value system. No matter what our expressed individual intentions may be, we still act primarily on the basis of ingrained systems of thought that reflect our culture. Indeed such "socialization" guarantees the survival and functioning of the social order. Those who are not sufficiently guided by the values of their culture often must be placed in mental institutions or the equivalent. At the least they are regarded as deviates, rebels, or misfits.

Inevitably, cultural perceptions tend to shape all that we think, say, and do, and racism in the United States— the hatred of that which is black—is part of our cultural value system. My wife often recounts instances of her own unconscious, culturally conditioned racism, or antiblack feelings, even now that she is a black homemaker and upholder *par excellence* of black pride. She explains that, when she hears a group of white children making too much noise, her reaction is simply, "Those children should be more quiet." When she hears a group of black children doing the same thing, her instant reaction is threefold. First, there is a feeling of condemnation: "Those terribly noisy black kids!" A split second later there is revulsion toward white America for what it has taught *even her* in terms of self-hatred. Then, just as quickly, there is the counsel of maturity: "Now, Barbara, be sane and wise."

Among black people self-hatred—the unconscious, culturally conditioned hatred of that which is black—drives distraught men, women, and children to self-destruction on the "dead-end streets" of our inner-city ghettos. Self-hatred is the black counterpart of the white racism that despises whatever is black in our society.

Look up "black" and "white" in the dictionary. Webster's *New World Dictionary: College Edition* (1964) defines black thus:

1. opposite to white . . . 2. dark-complexioned. 3. Negro . . . 4. totally without light; in complete darkness, dark. 5. soiled; dirty. 6. wearing black clothing. 7. evil, wicked, harmful. 8. disgraceful. 9. sad; dismal; gloomy . . . 10. sullen; angered. 11. without hope; as, a black future . . .

The same dictionary defines "white" in far different terms:

1. having the color of pure snow or milk; of the color of radiated, transmitted, or reflected light containing all the visible rays of the spectrum; opposite to black. 2. of a light or pale color; specifically, a) gray; silvery; hoary. b) very blond. c) pale; wan; pallid; ashen; as a face *white* with terror. d) light-yellow or amber; as, *white* wines. e) blank; said of a

page unmarked by printing, writing, etc. f) of a light-gray color and lustrous appearance; unburnished; said of silver and other metal. g) made of silver. h) snowy; as, a *white* Christmas. 3. clothed in white; wearing a white habit: as, the *White* Friars. 4. morally or spiritually pure; spotless; innocent. 5. free from evil intent; harmless; as *white* magic, a *white* lie. 6. (rare) happy; fortunate; auspicious; said of times and seasons. 7. a) having a light-colored skin; Caucasian. b) of or controlled by the white race; as, *white* supremacy. c) (nations of racial superiority). (slang), honest, fair, dependable. 8. being at white heat . . . 9. reactionary, counter-revolutionary, or royalist, as opposed to *red* (radical or revolutionary) . . .

Black people start off with two strikes—cultural bias and racism—against them, feelings of nonbeing, of negative identity.

Small wonder, then, that so much of our black urban youth has poor learning habits. Small wonder also that so many crimes of self-destruction and so many social and civic expressions of self-hatred occur!

The same American racism that drives black men to self-hatred provides the tragic subconscious expectation of black "nonlearning" among white teachers of black youth. David Gottlieb, in a study of attitudes of white and black teachers toward black pupils noted significant differences between the two groups. A. Harry Passow's observations on the study, in the Columbia University Teachers College pamphlet *Diminishing Teacher Prejudice* are revealing (the italics are mine):

When selecting from a list of 33 adjectives those which most accurately described their pupils in the inner-city schools, Negro and white teachers differed in their choices. In order of importance, white teachers most frequently selected talkative, lazy, fun lov-

ing, high strung and rebellious. Negro teachers selected fun loving, happy, cooperative, energetic and
ambitious. *The white teachers tended to omit adjectives which are universal attributes of children and
related to success.*

⌈The white community must recognize that our schools
are a particularly dangerous arena for the same racism
that the President's Commission on Civil Disorders has
described as pervading the nation's life. To remedy or
alleviate the condition in most of our cities—*if our primary goal is maximum human development*—several
practical steps must be taken.

— First, school boards—state, regional, and local—should
be made predominantly black; this step could benefit the
entire educational enterprise and would cost not one extra
cent! Whenever we look at the problems of black communities we see the problems of the United States as a
whole in dimensions clear and bold enough for all to
understand. The problems of black America are those of
white America in extreme form. To come to terms with
them will benefit all of us. Black people, whose pressing
immediate needs are also the basic long-range needs of
the whole nation, are the best available resource for improving our urban and semisuburban schools.

— Second, black leadership at the superintendent and as-
sistant-superintendent levels is essential. White teachers
—and white society in general—desperately need estima-
ble black models of authority. Furthermore, as black communities have tended to send some of their most gifted
people into education (white communities have tended to
send their brightest people into business), black leadership realistically ought to preponderate in our national
educational enterprise.

Ability to accomplish the necessary tasks must be recognized as the only rational criterion for selecting adminis-

trative, as well as teaching, personnel. Clear examples of black success at high levels would also furnish the hope needed to eliminate "nonlearning" among hopeless black urban youth. Arbitrary course-credit requirements for personnel qualification are already given less importance in our better suburban schools than in our urban schools. Arbitrary administrative criteria for teacher certification and promotion must be abolished as an effective, even though usually unintended, racist mechanism for keeping blacks from achieving high posts in our schools.

The third step should be to concede to the most capable and candid black consultants the primary planning responsibilities for those urban schools that have mainly black student bodies and increasingly unmet needs. The advantages of this suggestion should be self-evident. Spending for good consultation is the most economical measure our school systems may adopt. In my own experience as an urban-affairs and educational consultant I have found that even many seemingly well-intentioned white people are hesitant to learn survival techniques from men and women whose credentials are precisely those required in our cities and our schools if these men and women happen to be black. Yet, if we are to overcome the massive "nonlearning" that is eroding the foundations of our nation, white men must learn quickly to seek out and listen to competent black advisers.

The story of our cities in general and of our city schools in particular is like the oft-repeated tale of the man who is told that he must either face surgery or die: His obituary omits the cause of death as "The failure to face reality." Programs for overcoming racism—on the state and local levels—can best be developed by trained and candid black men and women. The physician chosen because he tells his patients what they want to hear is a physician chosen by a fool. Some resource should be added to the available literature for our schools when work with which

I am engaged with Dr. Frederick Hahn at Upsala College in conjunction with the East Orange, New Jersey, public schools is published early in 1969.

— Fourth, self-awareness among teachers is essential. Even where massive upgrading of black teachers is possible as part of an effort to overcome the effects of racism, programs to develop teacher self-awareness should also be provided. They must be part of teacher-training programs and of in-service programs within the schools. Black teachers tend to be more aware of the common low-status needs of all who are black. Harry Passow notes their tendency to be protective of black students. In urban schools white teachers who come from blue-collar backgrounds tend especially to be threatened by the presence of those who remind them of the social or economic backgrounds from which they have sought to escape. The lower-class white children in our urban schools, along with the black children who symbolize low socioeconomic status, become for some teachers invisible students who cannot be taught. To the teacher caught in this bind the presence of an identity threat—in the children—is simply wished away. Teachers cannot teach pupils whom they have "wished away."

Two basic attributes are necessary for good teaching: understanding of oneself and knowledge and love of one's subject. Failure to understand and accept oneself is the basic barrier to all communication. A person who does not know or accept himself cannot know or accept others.

On the other hand, one who knows and accepts himself can relate freely to others. Our teachers are the primary guardians of our young outside the home. The kind of reality—or unreality—that the teacher creates in the classroom is perhaps the greatest single social instrument for shaping the future character of the nation. State and local governments must be encouraged by their citizens to promote continual in-service training for teachers to help them understand themselves better. In a racist society, everyone *tends* to be racist. Those who are not sufficiently self-aware to recognize this cultural conditioning and the continuing need to control its manifestations are in serious trouble. Indeed, every business, religious, governmental, and civic institution must undertake such self-examination if we are to overcome the racism that lies at the heart of our urban distress.

The fifth and perhaps most difficult task in overcoming racism in schools is also the most vital. Staff realignments of a radical nature are called for in many of our schools. Repressive principals, guidance counselors, teachers, secretaries, and higher-echelon administrative personnel should be replaced. Where overt damage is being done, there is no other choice.

The Ford Motor Company would replace any executive or clerk or craftsman whose work tended to produce faulty cars; any responsibly run enterprise in the nation would take similar action. Are motor cars more important than people? In the end, only a deeply concerned and responsible citizenry can guarantee that our schools fulfill their sacred trust.

Stop the Plunder

In far too many municipalities schools are used as sources of patronage, as political power bases. The great contribution of the Bundy plan for the decentralization of the New York City schools is recognition that schools should be managed in substantial measure by those whose children's needs they serve.

A serious problem, which we have failed to face squarely in any city in the nation, is deciding on the degree to which those who do not have children in the public schools should manage or serve the public schools. Admittedly, there are no easy answers. Yet it is obvious that our failure even to face this problem has been the source of much of what Joseph Alsop calls a "catastrophic failure" of our schools to serve many of the needs of its constituents. Those whose interests are most remote from those of the students must occupy a rapidly diminishing place in the operation and management of our public education. And Americans must recognize—as do people in most other major nations—that the public has a major continuing responsibility for the education and nurture of its youth, regardless of the type of educational institutions adopted.

Joseph Alsop, in a syndicated column (February 21, 1968), wrote: "The majority in this country has not merely failed, quickly, shockingly and catastrophically, to offer justice and equal opportunity to the Negro minority. At the moment, the white majority is also being flabbily self-deluding about the real consequences of their own failure." Mr. Alsop predicts, as a consequence, a growing tendency toward a "direct-action campaign to seize the schools themselves." He quotes Stokely Carmichael as saying, "We intend by any means necessary to take over the school system [in Washington] so that it will respond to black people's needs." Mr. Alsop goes on to remind his readers, "Control of the schools by the parents is an accepted American principle." He is fearful, however, that unless the white people who now hold the reins in our urban schools are far more responsive to the educational needs of our black communities, extremism of a dangerous kind may be the demoralizing result. Mr. Alsop concludes with this warning to the white majority (the italics are mine): "This desperately dangerous situation has arisen *because ghetto schools do not in fact give ghetto children a decent education.* And we shall surely have apartheid in America one day, *unless the white majority* joins in supporting a massive, general, very costly nationwide program of ghetto school-improvement."

Our schools are intended to educate the young. Yet at

present they are more successful in providing gainful employment and a stage for political maneuvering among people whose immediate interests are clearly unrelated to those of the children whom the schools are supposed to educate. We must somehow stop the sideshow and get on—in the most reasonable and effective ways possible— with the tragically neglected business of providing the fullest and best education possible for our nation's most wantonly wasted human resource, our inner-city black youth.

Teach!

Psychologist Kenneth Clark declares:

> A normal child who is expected to learn, *who is taught* and who is required to learn will learn. . . . A single standard of academic expectations, a demanding syllabus, and *skillful and understanding teaching* are essential to the raising of the self-esteem of disadvantaged children, increasing their motivation for academic achievement and providing our society with the benefits of their intellectual potential.

What Dr. Clark calls for seems simple enough on the surface. Yet the motivation to turn others on to learning depends in substantial measure upon the social insights and views of reality possessed by those who teach. A teacher cannot "turn pupils on" if he sees in them threatening reminders of a personal past that he wishes to forget. Nor can he turn pupils on—quicken their sense of worth, importance, hope, and determination—if he fears that to do so will create undesirable social or economic consequences. In one school system in which I worked a few years ago a teacher remarked that she "had to" fail most of the pupils in one academic course for college-bound students simply because the colleges didn't have enough room for the youngsters whom she taught. In a group of some twenty people not one ripple of dissent greeted this remark.

Teachers are, in fact, social scientists and social planners of a sort. They give more guidance counseling than do parents and trained guidance counselors combined. We must face the fact that, in order to motivate pupils to learn, teachers must have a sense of social purpose. What is the social purpose of a teacher in a society that only now has begun—through its Presidential Commission on Civil Disorders—to examine its pervasive racism? Clearly a teacher's kindness, dedication, good will, and good sense are inseparable from the cultural values that he is sworn to impart to his pupils. This interrelationship creates absolute impossibilities for our teachers. For, the harder they try in an unconsciously racist society, the more devastating will be their results, especially in our black-populated urban schools. A kindhearted teacher who is not mindful of her unconscious culturally rooted, anti-black values will simply be anti-black in a sweet and unconscious way.

Our teachers would not have it this way if they could choose. *Every institution in our society must concentrate immediately upon an examination of our value system* and must share in a national assessment of how that system may be updated to meet the needs created by the rapidly changing times that are upon us.

In business, government, and social and civic agencies—as well as in education and the churches—I meet deeply dedicated people who may be described as unconsciously "doing the devil's work." They see our social order as largely unchanging and, with the deepest personal regrets and travail of conscience, feel that much of human life must be wasted. This passivity is perhaps one of the greatest tragedies of our society.

Somehow we must come to see that institutions were

made to serve man, rather than the reverse, and that the purpose of life is to use to the fullest all the gifts with which every man is endowed. As Dr. Clark suggests, when pupils are motivated and taught, they can and will learn and so provide our society "with the benefits of their intellectual potential."

Expect the Best!

Vernon Haubrich believes that many of the practical difficulties of teachers in inner-city schools revolve around their inability to emphathize, to enter imaginatively into the life experiences of their pupils. He says that their approach is marked by the "inability to comprehend, understand, and cope with the multiple problems of language development, varying social norms, habits not accepted by the teacher, behavior which is often not success-oriented, lack of student cooperation, and achievement levels well below expectancies of pupils."

One of the great teachers at Terrace Park High School, located just outside the Cincinnati, Ohio, city limits, was Mrs. Louis Butterfield Foster. The Foster family—like my mother's family, the Hickmans—had lived in the Cincinnati area for more than 100 years. Mrs. Foster's ancestors had been leaders in the underground-railway movement, in which escaped slaves were hidden and assisted toward safety and freedom. The spirit of redemption, the release of human energies to realize human potential, was a deeply ingrained part of the Foster family's value system. Whenever a black student encountered academic difficulty—or presented a disciplinary problem—Mrs. Foster could almost always be counted on to set things back on their proper course.

I have known many white teachers whose liberated social outlook and vision of human fulfillment were in the same basic tradition; they have required the best from life and recognize only the best in those about them. More

of our teachers today need such role models to enable
them to view life in a way that would turn what is presently daily drudgery into satisfying effort.

Teachers, to become thus liberated, need to relate,
either actually or symbolically, to those whom they would
teach. Both my mother and my grandmother were school
teachers. They were motivated by the recognition that
upon what they and others like them accomplished depended the survival and status of their race. They had
something immediate to lose in every failure and something immediate to gain in every success. All our teachers
should have a similar sense that our national survival and
that of the human race depend largely upon what they
accomplish in terms of encouraging human self-fulfillment.

Teachers who view their task in such a way will not
find disciplinary problems so formidable. I do not accept,
personally or professionally, the thesis that better teacher-
pupil or teacher-parent relations are at the heart of the
growing dislocations in our schools. Our parents and
teachers do urgently need far more help, guidance, and
cooperation. Interpretation of the best kind is called for.
Fundamentally, however, we must develop in our parents
and teachers—and through them in our pupils—a new
vision of what life *is* and of what it must for the sake of
the nation's destiny *become*.

Those of our citizens in business, in churches, and in
social and civic agencies must develop new patterns of
cooperation to undergird and improve the work that our
most dedicated teachers and school administrators are
seeking to accomplish.

A reporter in one New England city, Howard Abram-
son, wrote a series of articles in the New Haven *Journal-
Courier* about growing unrest in the schools, in which he
said:

According to many black students, the teachers are

one of the major causes of their unrest. It was the teacher's bigotry or ignorance that made them lash out violently, they claimed.

To the parent, it has become convenient to blame the teacher, either because the parent unquestionably believes the words of his student-child or, perhaps, because the teacher is in the most vulnerable position —the middle.

During last summer's racial violence throughout the country, it was said by many that the Negro wasn't attacking the neighborhood policeman because he was who he was; they were attacking him because he was the symbol of the white power structure that had retarded the Negro's escape from the ghetto and from poverty itself.

The teacher, like the policeman, implements, not originates, policy. They both represent, perhaps at the lowest echelon, their respective administrations. Both have neither the power to appreciably and directly change the policy they implement, nor the loftiness of office to hide behind a closed door or an official press release.

The teachers, almost unanimously, feel the cause of school violence is a basic breakdown in the discipline of the students.

Most view it as a breakdown of discipline in all phases of life, not just in the schools. The blame must be shared, though perhaps not equally, between the parents, teachers and society itself, it was generally agreed.

This article reflects the fact that our teachers need new relationships with the parents of their students. They should be far more closely involved in the immediate circumstances of their students' lives. Teachers must also both have and recognize positive personal stakes in success with every student. More fundamentally, recognition of the changes in our society that make it imperative that all students be fully developed must be accepted as the responsibility of government, business, civic, and religious agencies and of all our community leaders.

⌊It should be apparent that our teachers cannot do their best when they, their students, and the parents do not understand that, in the world that has suddenly evolved, all our institutions and systems of order must be adapted to necessary and continuous social change. Otherwise, discipline appears as repression, and the call for order is viewed as one more evidence of the pernicious, if unconscious, racism that pervades the nation's life.⌉

Nor can we teach our children at the same time that we shame them, albeit unconsciously. Sociologist Howard Becker, in a study of teacher attitudes in the Chicago schools, found that most teachers believed that slum children were "difficult to teach" and "morally unacceptable on all scores." I recently visited a community in upstate New York and was asked by one teacher just how she might go about teaching English more effectively to the black children in her classes. "I noticed," she explained, "how you move back and forth between Harvardian English and 'soul talk'; and, quite frankly, I was absolutely delighted! I now wonder whether I should not encourage our black children to continue to use their 'soul talk' in their conversation outside the classroom instead of shaming them as I have actually done. . . . Perhaps in this way, I could teach them better." Her logic seemed irresistible.

Dr. Anna Hedgeman says that it was the late Harry Burleigh who first taught her to appreciate the use of black dialect. He pointed out to her that the use of dialect —or subcultural argot—reflects the effort of people to communicate the otherwise hidden and neglected but nonetheless precious truths of their inner worlds. It represents a people's struggle for identity and integrity, and it must not be laughed off.

The Germans grew accustomed, over a period of generations, to the use of "high" German in the courts and at the post office, whereas local dialects, which were respected by all, abounded in daily conversation. In India, there are a score of languages and hundreds of dialects. In our uncritical drive toward uniformity throughout the nation, we mix great harm with apparent good. Our teachers cannot teach black children by unconsciously deprecating the latter's struggle for being or by conveying negative judgments of parents who possibly can speak only argot.

It is not the responsibility of the schools, however, to teach argot. Their classroom task is to prepare their children to deal most competently with the norms or standards of our middle-class controlled and oriented life. For teachers or school administrators to scorn the preparation of black children for competence in a middle-class world is to will their failure to survive. The sudden and ostensibly helpful desire of white administrators and educational planners to "experiment" with black children's needs must be viewed against the background of unconscious racism in the nation's life. Lack of perception of the true needs of the black community may lead even those of the greatest good will to a disaster. Black planners are the people best qualified to plan for those whose fortunes are most closely tied to their own. For this same reason, they also might be used for *most* basic social planning. Are not the needs of our black youth, though far greater, still the same as the needs of our youth in general?

Our Colleges and Universities

"If you were the president of a white college of the size and nature of this one," a college president recently asked me, "what would you do to improve its racial situation?"

The question was a good one, and I threw it back to him to answer for himself. He paused for a moment and then said, "I think I would seek out some competent advice." He could not have given a better answer. In every agency in our society, in which past cultural perceptions have shaped our common and personal life, we should solicit the most competent advice and assistance that we can get. Otherwise, we shall founder.

A friend of mine recently told of his experience as an official adviser on racial matters for one institution of higher learning. He had no direct communication with the president but communicated with the administration only through a member of the teaching staff. The school, without the knowledge or help of its official black adviser, sought the opinions of all kinds of black people, gathering a kind of smorgasbord of information, in which his own advice was merely one more element, from which the administration might as well have chosen according to whim or fancy.

His experience is unfortunately all too representative. Competent advice must be seriously sought and responsibly received. It cannot be taken lightly if our private and public agencies are to make necessary adjustments in these changing times.

Discovery of Truth

[American colleges are in trouble in many ways, not least among which is their failure to develop or disseminate adequately the knowledge essential to meeting the challenges that we as a nation face.]

Knowledge of truth is never more than partial, but listening to people of different ages, cultural backgrounds, and historical perspectives may extend our perceptions of truth. Understanding history is particularly important, and, as we saw in Chapter 2, significant omissions in teaching our country's history have contributed heavily though indirectly to our current social unrest. Our institutions of higher learning have the responsibility of helping to correct such distortions of the past.

In more immediate terms, our colleges and universities cannot claim to further the search for truth if their own faculties do not accurately reflect and represent the nation's entire cultural experience. Black faculty members should be expressly sought for their specific historical and cultural perspectives and insights, which are indispensable to developing the broadest possible truth.

This point was emphasized for me a few years ago while I was browsing through the stacks at Harvard's Widener Library. In the economics section my eye fell on the name of Gunnar Myrdal. I was a bit surprised, as I knew only his work in sociology, through his classic study of America's black population, *An American Dilemma*. But he is, after all, an economist. I opened the book, which dealt with the economic development of underdeveloped nations, and in the first few pages Dr. Myrdal made the following point: As economics is a theoretical study and as such requires constant extension and rethinking, we make a mistake by simply teaching students from other cultures our theories. We should share our analytical tools as well and let them enrich our body of theory with their fresh perspectives.

Every institution of higher learning should recognize this logic. The faculties of all our schools cannot continue to be homogeneous in cultural or racial backgrounds and hope to deal most responsibly with truth. Where vacancies occur, in both significant teaching and administrative posts, black men of candor and competence who have assimilated and integrated their own subcultural values should be deliberately sought to fill them. Such men must be esteemed as necessary additions to the staffs and faculties of our schools, in which until now students have clearly been deprived of access to the broadest possible perspectives on truth.

In much the same spirit, if schools are to provide our youth with the first-hand experience that will equip them to deal most competently with the future, young people of varying backgrounds must also be sought out as full-fledged four-year students. In view of our admittedly racist mores, there should also be a deliberate effort to make every aspect of student government as racially inclusive as possible. To accomplish these purposes, scholarship aid and other special opportunities must be greatly expanded.

University departments that train students specifically for work in urban affairs are clearly deficient if their staffs do not include black people who are especially familiar with and sensitive to some of the most wide-spread urban needs. Cities are people, and the black people in our cities experience urban needs in the most direct and urgent way. For the immediate peace and safety of the nation, urban planning must become more "people-oriented"; it must therefore be conducted by, and with the advice of, the best black minds that the nation has available. Schools of social work and education must also see their needs, opportunities, and responsibilities in this light.

Continuing Education

Our four-year colleges should be multiplied. But, far more important, a new system of Federally financed two-year colleges, extending into every community of the land, should be established.

The issue of Federal versus local control of education might take on a different, less controversial, dimension if the Federal government exercised less direct control over expenditures for the lower grades but provided major funds and direction for a massive and urgently needed adult-education enterprise instead.

Needs for career training and retraining and our obvious failure to provide sufficient arts education for the masses of our adults make it mandatory that our Federal government provide for these needs. Unless such an enterprise takes place on the college level and is oriented to local needs—including compensatory training—it cannot hope to accomplish its task. Most people in the days ahead will need at least two years of education beyond high school, with built-in rewards and the opportunity to return repeatedly.

Our present institutions of higher education have traditionally been geared to the needs of leisured adults. Today leisured urbanites are largely welfare clients and growing numbers of idle black males. In providing vehicles to meet their immediate needs, we may also provide for other, long-standing needs of our society as a whole. For example, early retirement will increase the need for retraining in vocational and other skills. For a travel- and recreation-minded population there should be schools that give credit courses in the history and culture of regions of our own country and other parts of the world, along with recreation (sports history, nature studies for the outdoorsman) and hobby skills. An old truism must be revived: "Education is for the needs of man, not man for the needs of education."

Our higher education—along with our public schools—should be redirected toward meeting the needs of all in a period of rapidly accelerating change. We cannot afford to find ourselves caught in the dilemma of the man who complained that he could never quite determine whether it was preferable to say with honesty, "I *is* rich" or "I *am* poor."

The only concerns that should condition our planning

are those that reflect the need to develop the unused talents of every citizen. Education must always be adapted to fit the practical needs of our times.

In this way, our schools will keep their trust as guardians of youth and rekindle the lamps of learning where they burn too low for our common safety and security.

CHAPTER FIVE

Twenty Tasks
for White People

WILLIAM BOOTH, CHAIRMAN OF THE NEW YORK CITY
Commission on Human Rights, recently told a group of
business executives:

> I happen to be one of those who have perhaps
> greater confidence in what you are doing for "the
> cause" than many of you do. It is my feeling—and
> that of many others—that one of the major "coolants"
> in last year's long, hot summer was the National Con-
> ference on Black Power. That conference could not
> have taken place had it not been for both the support
> in part and neutralization in part of many of you in
> the business community. I have no doubt that the per-
> son most responsible for achieving this has been one
> with whom many of us have worked and have had to
> respect.

Without many hands, both black and white, working
cooperatively, hardly any major task to further the nation's
peaceable and orderly development can be accomplished.
Hundreds of people, both white and black, working in

their own way, were required to achieve this precarious first step toward an urgently needed new operational harmony and communication among black people: the National Conference on Black Power. The one person to whom Mr. Booth referred, among the hundreds of people who played an invaluable part in bringing the conference about, was my twin brother Benjamin. He is an economist who works with business and industrial leaders day and night, hammering home his prophetic message that both the immediate and long-range interests of business are tied up with the achievement of justice for all. A sound economy can rest only on the foundation of a peaceful and productive nation. Business must therefore do everything within its power to create an environment conducive to continuous and orderly progress for every segment of our society.

The message that Ben Wright carries to white business and civic leadership can be summed up in what he has catalogued as "twenty tasks." The tasks necessarily involve overlaps, as they are designed to appeal to as wide a range of interests as possible. His own summation of each task for white people is italicized in the following discussion.

1. *Study your own historically rooted role in the vast amount of racism that exists in America today by* (a) *requiring that Negro and African history and culture be taught in our school systems at all levels;* (b) *encouraging church groups, cultural groups, civic organizations, etc., to have series of discussions on American history in relation to black people so that adults will also learn to understand themselves.*

Black history should and must be taught in all our schools. Its present exclusion is one more denial of reality for black people and has the same effect as the uncon-

sciously racist, supposedly "objective" governmental and
social-scientific use of the term "nonwhite" to refer to
black people. Indeed, the suggestion of only a few influ-
ential white men could eliminate from governmental and
social-science usage the unhelpful term "nonwhite." It is a
historically rooted part of the American mentality to exclude from its vision of reality those who are black. Under
such conditions, it is almost inevitable that, when a businessman thinks of hiring or promotion, he tends to exclude
from consideration those whom he does not "see." To ac-
cuse individual businessmen of deliberate discrimination
may often be unjust. Their intentions may be exemplary.
But, in an environment like the one described by the President's Commission on Civil Disorders as characteristic of
this nation, the best-intentioned behavior will most likely
reflect the dishonest assumptions at the foundation of
society.

We must work to change the common definition of who
we as a nation are if we are to function in the most efficient and democratic way today. There is today no purpose and no logic to justify classification in the Federal
Census of 20 per cent of our population as different from
the rest. The unique and rich heritage of black people
affords no justification for the census takers to set them off,
effectively, as non-American. Yet the common legacy of
American history as it is taught throughout the nation is
the assumption that white people are the "us," the most
truly American; the rest are "others."

Those whose own interests are tied up with achieving
the most productive life possible for everyone in the nation—as well as those who simply feel a civic responsibility to help the United States to fulfill the promises
on which it was founded—must see to it that our working
assumptions are corrected. Our business and financial
leaders exercise the greatest power over most of our population in both day-to-day and long-range decision making.

In a matter of months, given the will, a mere handful of dedicated, enlightened, and determined business leaders—with the help of competent black advisers and public-relations aides—could bring about a basic shift in our racist patterns of thought and activity.

Raymond Brown, long a worker for justice and power for black people and perhaps New Jersey's ablest criminal lawyer, describes how both legal and political decisions are most often determined by the pressures, overt and subtle, of only those few men in every community who wield financial power. He always defends black students and other black militants against criticism for using "fairy-tale language" in referring to the "power structure" of our cities, states, and nation. Our social scientists and historians, too, have over the years identified "the kingmakers" and those who silently govern. And those who execute the commands of power know well whose voices they must heed.

Our unofficial decision makers and those who have the greatest contact with them *can* see to it that our distorted view of America is radically altered quickly enough to avoid disaster. Black history, both as merely black history and as an integral part of our total history, must be added to our public- and private-school curricula. Both black and white youngsters have been systematically exposed to a distorted "lily white" image of America, as part of, and support for, our deeply rooted racist culture patterns. This distortion must be corrected. Perhaps in a far more basic way, as we shall see in later discussion of what black people must do for themselves, black values are necessary for the reform of the nation's life. Without them, we may well be lost as a nation. The series of advertisements called "Ingenious Americans," in which National Distillers Inc., makers of Old Taylor whiskey, publicize black heroes in *Ebony* should be made available to the general public. Such companies as National Distillers deserve applause, and their example must be continuously repeated by many others. Even more important, however, as we shall see, is that American business and industry—along with civic, governmental, and religious agencies—should shift gears radically in their employment and advancement patterns. In this way, we may make each new day a better part of history.

   2. Associate yourselves with thinking black people who accept their own blackness. In this way, black people in every enterprise, rather than simply being imbued with the thinking current in the system that has brought us to our present chaos, can contribute creatively to that thinking.

It is a truism that we cannot realize our best selves by trying to be carbon copies of others. Our goal in the past has been to train black people to conform to the prevailing trends in white America. Yet, in our present national distress, it should be apparent that new and untried perceptions must be examined and used for their potential good.

The Department of Education at Upsala College in East Orange, New Jersey, recently sought the participation, in an all-day brain-storming session, of a group of black intellectuals and skilled professionals who are in tune with the growing mood of black militance and self-awareness. A group of white educators also participated. We first met in racial groups to examine our culturally conditioned perceptions of the needs and opportunities confronting urban education. Then the entire body joined in a general session, to which reports were made by both groups. After lunch, the groups were arbitrarily mixed, or integrated, and a general reporting session concluded the day.

Afterward Dr. Frederick Hahn, Director of Elementary Education at Upsala College, explained:

A whole new world of reality was opened to me. Several months before our meeting I would have found abhorrent even the idea that there was any substantial difference between white and black teachers or pupils. I had always subscribed to the idea that an American and an idealist must somehow be "color blind." I thought that I was prepared for any eventuality before our unusual session. But I wasn't. I thought for one thing that I was an entirely open-minded white man; and I found it hard to take when there was some seeming doubt about this expressed by those in the black meeting. As the group reports came in, I recognized that these black people, who saw themselves as having essentially different historical and cultural ingredients in their experience as black men had some far different—and yet completely logical—perceptions to add to those which I had of my teaching situation.

One of our older white consultants, Dr. Louis Raths, complained openly that he had been in the educational and urban planning business for many years. "But where," he asked, "have they been keeping such open and honest Negroes like this?" He felt greatly helped, and so was quite disappointed that over the years he had not benefitted from such candid and creative thinking. That was a memorable and deeply rewarding day.

The new mood of black self-awareness can contribute to every enterprise of which black people are a part by affording fresh insights that otherwise might not be available. Black people who are aware of their own rich cultural experience must be encouraged—and aggressively sought out—to bring new perspectives to bear in every problem area that we face. "The same tune, second verse" may prove to be a lingering death song. But new insights may bring new hope.

Dr. Hahn, in reviewing the tapes of his meeting noticed, among many suggestions for radical alterations in his program of teacher education, the repeated use—in a context that evoked new understanding—of such terms as "finding one's identity," "empowerment," "unconscious influence of historical perceptions," and "teacher self-interest in pupil success." Like many other planners who have really listened to black people, he was "turned on" and plans to engage in some long-postponed writing for which that one experience provided the missing ingredients.

3. *Recognize that governments are not meant to be efficiency systems for building robots but should be "people-oriented" or "community-oriented" enterprises in which the people affected are consulted on—and are in some large measure in control of—urban-renewal programs and other efforts designed to meet their needs.*

For Richard Bell, President of the Board of Directors of the Community Council of Greater New Haven, it was a real discovery that black people in his city had so little control over even the most immediate of their own concerns. "New Haven—and every large community where black people live—is remarkably like the old plantations," explained a local social group work agency official: "White people decide the details of our daily life." "The one big but simple issue before us," says Minister Kariem, soft-spoken leader of New Haven's Black Muslim mosque, "is that of who will control the destinies of black people?"

Edward Geyer, rector of St. Luke's Church in New Haven, believes that acceptance of white control over

black lives in some cities has a parallel in the docility of
the slaves in the Roman Empire. The status of Roman
slaves depended on the status of their masters. In New
Haven, black people have survived fairly well, even those
whose highest ambition has been to wait tables at the
city's exclusive clubs, to teach school, or to work in the
post office. The white people, who have engineered the
physical renewal of downtown New Haven and the destruction of the heart of the black community, have given
black people the feeling that they were going to be living
in a "nigger heaven." "When lulled to sleep," Father
Geyer says, "it is hard to get momentum. We are indebted
to the so-called 'militants' for at least sounding an overdue alarm."

Not long ago I went to a major city and spoke before
the leaders of the white business community. Almost always businessmen respond most favorably to the message
that larger markets depend upon a prosperous and peaceable population. I am therefore almost invariably well
received when I speak before white business leaders. In
this particular city, however, one businessman was evi-
dently so threatened by his image of black power that he
could not recognize the relatively conservative tones that
marked my presentation. He launched into a tirade and
then demanded to know whether the black men present
agreed with him or with me. Present in the room were
white businessmen and the black men immediately responsible to them either in business or social agencies.
The only black man who would speak up in support of my
message was a state senator, elected by black people.
The others, who were in almost the same position as kept
women, either remained silent or voiced opinions acceptable to the businessmen who were the major source of their
own immediate status.

White leaders, if they are to benefit from competent
black advice, will have to seek out black men whose im-

mediate livelihoods are not at stake. It is tragically true
that far too many black people labor under the illusion
that conformity breeds security. It is not good for business, nor is it good for the nation, for the plantation mentality to continue. Trained black men must recognize that
their worth to their employers increases as their honesty,
their frankness, and their acceptance of their own unique
black heritage increase. Those white people who are both
thoughtful and responsible will insist that those black
people who presently act as if they were enslaved learn to
think and act as free men for the sake of simple survival
for us all. They will also re-examine their own unconscious, historically rooted tendency to perpetuate the
plantation mentality even when their expressed will is in
the opposite direction.

*4. Examine or re-examine our educational system
to see if it is meeting the needs of whites and blacks
in the light of the vastly different and continually
changing economic and social conditions in our country. White people must realize that, if they don't force
some radical changes in our educational system, it is
they who will carry the primary burden of increased
taxes for welfare, police and fire protection, and the
incalculable costs of continued urban unrest.*

C. Sumner ("Chuck") Stone tells of his most frustrating
daily task as administrative aide to Congressman Adam
Clayton Powell, bucking his head against the backsides of
ostriches with their heads buried in the sand. "The nation's real feelings about the security of its own institutions," he says, "can be seen as plain as day in the greater
eagerness to suspend any and all rules to 'get Adam' than
to pursue the good which he was doing uniquely for the
future of education along with many other things."
Black people, in their rising revolt in our cities, are

speaking for the interests of all who would keep the United States strong and healthy and free. The fact that our institutions have not worked to produce the good life for what is now far more than "one-fifth of the nation" should suggest to the sober and wise that we must shake off our lethargy if growing *rigor mortis* is not to paralyze our entire society.

Why don't others join us? is the great mystery to overwhelming numbers of black people. Bayard Rustin wonders why the white poor do not see their cause as identical with that of their black brothers. Dr. Ann Fried of the New York City Mission Society and Mrs. Grace Malone, director of Newark's Public Welfare, form a kind of informal biracial team that has worked hard though quietly to persuade white leaders that what black people are demanding will not benefit themselves alone or even primarily but will also serve the immediate good of those who happen to be white. The Stones, the Rustins, the Frieds, and the Malones all are working for basic structural changes in our society.

5. *Recruit and train better men to police our cities for the good of both white and black. To allow an uneducated policeman or uniformed person to make professional human-relations decisions just won't work.*

Herbert Scott is an assistant city prosecutor. He is black. He wonders why our white-controlled society will not come to the aid of the officers of the peace in an enlightened and determined way. "It is time that someone started speaking up for real law and order," he says. The police are given jobs to do that call for far greater training than the public requires them to have. "The police have more authority over life and death than does the President of the United States," says Roger Alling, a white colleague in the Newark office where I work. "The police may in effect declare a court of special session at any time or any place and then serve as judge, jury, and executioner in a decision of life or death."

Surely today our policemen should have a new and vastly different image, as "officers of the peace," and should receive far greater pay and training. In more disturbed areas where racial unrest runs high, if our purpose is to maintain the peace, we must use somewhat different resources than those we have used in the past. Reports on past civil disorders suggest that the people who are successful in maintaining the peace in periods of upheaval are those who are perceived as advocates rather than as adversaries by the rebellious. Jersey City's Raymond Brown, Dudley Sarfaty of the New Jersey Synod of the Presbyterian Church, and members of the Diocese of Newark staff have together been advancing the idea that unemployed males in potentially explosive areas be recruited, trained, deputized, and paid as unarmed officers of the peace. Such men are advocates for their neighbors, and they need employment. The cost? Would it not be self-liquidating? Civil-defense funds and other available moneys and resources could be used for this kind of endeavor. In every state and municipality, efforts should be made in this direction. Informal committees should be established for this purpose.

Perhaps most important, efforts of a concentrated nature must be made immediately to change the qualifications for and credentials of our most forgotten public servants. The New Jersey Governor's Select Commission on civil disorders reports that of the thousands of municipal policemen in the state of New Jersey only a few have two years or more of college training. In Newark, New Jersey, of approximately 1,500 men, including officers and inspectors, ten have associate degrees, twelve have bachelors' degrees, and two have graduate training. This is only one example reflecting the grossest irresponsibility on the part of our society. Those who must make the most critical judgments in the keeping of the peace and in deciding over life or death should be the best trained. The public could well afford to pay for substantial collegiate training programs for all of our officers of the peace in that the social costs thereby reduced would far outweigh the upgrading expense. Further, our nation is entitled to the best in law enforcement; and the peace of our cities makes such an endeavor essential.

   6. *Support programs for self-development of black people. As long as black Americans do not join together to carry their full load in this nation and be rewarded justly, many of their responsibilities will rest on the shoulders of white America.*

In a caucus of black churchmen during the summer of 1967, at a meeting held under the auspices of the National Council of Churches, the conviction was expressed that the most notable white Christian in America during 1967 was the Episcopal Bishop of Newark, Leland Stark. He has never been told of this comment; indeed, in view of the hostile response of white America to the growing rebellion among black people, public notice of his work in 1967 could have compromised his work. Now that the report of the President's Commission on Civil Disorders is out, there may be far greater acceptance and appreciation of the efforts of those white leaders who seek—as did Bishop Stark in his refusal to stand in the way of the National Conference on Black Power—to advance the cause of fulfillment for all Americans. The National Conference on Black Power had its headquarters in the Episcopal Cathedral House in Newark. "I do not like the term 'black power,'" says Bishop Stark, "but that is not within my province to change. I do not see, however, how any reasonable person could be other than supportive of any realistic effort for the empowerment of black Americans." Dean Ledlie Laughlin of Newark's Trinity Cathedral explained to his officers and people that the presence of distinguished black men and women who were seeking to move America forward in new directions should be a welcome, even though surprising, circumstance.

Such support is needed on every hand and is within the capacity of all of us to give. On September 3, 1967, Dr. Carroll Simcox, in the face of much uninformed criticism, wrote an editorial in *Living Church*, which defended the "black power" movement and those of its leaders who were working to advance the nation's peace:

American history is very largely made up of achievements of this sort. This is a land of minorities. Every ethnic or cultural group in it can say, as the Israelites said: "We were strangers in the land of Egypt." Every one of these, the Anglo-Saxon element not excluded, began its American career as an afflicted minority. It moved on and moved up to a better life as it discovered and employed the strength that there is in union.

All advocates of black power, violent or non-violent, agree on one point: that if American Negroes are to climb they must do their own climbing; no one else will do it for them. They have a lot of history—all of it, in fact—supporting their thesis.

When Dr. Wright was in Chicago recently to help to form a Chicago black power committee, he declared that the black power program he is working to develop "is in no sense of the word anti-white." Its only purpose is to speak to "the problems, opportunities, and needs of the black community." Commenting on the causes of riots, he said that one of these "comes from a failure . . . on the part of black America to overcome the slave mentality of dependence upon others and their failure to generate a sense of self-respect." In other words, "power" comes to Negroes, as to any other group, as they shake off a servile dependence upon others, as they learn to respect themselves, as they work together to gain their proper objectives.

This, then, is black power as very many Negro Christians conceive of it and promote it. Can any American who knows his own history, or can any Christian who searches his own conscience, cast a stone at this?

Henry Ford II is among the many notable leaders in the white community—others are Jack Greenberg of the Legal Defense Fund of the N.A.A.C.P. and Vice-President Hubert Humphrey—who have spoken up in support of power for black Americans to stand on their own and have defended their doing so under the banner of "black power."

It was good to see that the President's Commission on Civil Disorders did not succumb to the pressures of a few to make the movement for black power a scapegoat for "black irresponsibility." White people cannot lead under the banner of black power. What we lead may quickly die once our leadership is gone. But if they help to strengthen the natural processes of growth they may contribute to a flowering and prosperity in our society out of proportion to the resources applied to achieve it.

Father Henry Offer, S.S.J., a white priest who serves as Director of the Archdiocesan Urban Commission in Baltimore, is credited with being the major catalyst in the gathering of black professional leaders in Baltimore to consider the reasonableness of black power. "We are grateful to him and others like him," says the Reverend Frank Williams, pastor of the Metropolitan Methodist Church.

"Father Offer has helped make my work and that of my colleagues a lot less lonely and a great deal more effective by disarming many who would otherwise continue to oppose us or be unwilling to agree."

Sister Mary Patricia of the Urban Sisters of the Apostolate in Chicago is enthusiastic about the possibilities of black power: "I want everyone to become what they ought to be. This is what God wants, so I want it too. People need power, a wholesome identity and self-respect."

Many more black people would join the movement for black power and would donate their insights and experience to it if only sympathetic white people would work in their own communities to persuade those who still believe that "white makes right," that power and self-respect for black people are necessary. By this means the timid might be encouraged to join in this endeavor, which is vital to the peace of the nation.

7. Devise ways by which both the image of black people among others and among themselves will be improved. As long as black people are regarded by others and themselves as nothing or as "others," black people will have little opportunity or incentive to try to become anything more than a drain on our society.

When no black man is pastor of a local church, white children and adults continue to believe that God is white, that white men were meant to lead, and that black men can be leaders only in limited areas among black men. Black children and adults, by the same token, learn that God is white and that black men have only a limited place in the world. Racist patterns are pervasive in the nation. Black institutions tend to be regarded as temporary, as are most minority-group institutions. The American dream and ideal for every group are to be recognized as

part of the controlling majority. Leadership in a majority
institution is therefore a criterion of position and achievement in our society.

Our institutional life—educational, civic, business, religious, and governmental—tends to serve white purposes
and to be white-controlled. When black men are not
granted the same opportunities as are others and when
past injustices are not compensated for, we reinforce our
present patterns of national self-destruction.

William Sayre, an eminent lawyer and churchman in
Montclair, New Jersey, says that white America has not
so much deliberately failed to fulfill its responsibilities as
it has failed to *recognize* them; it has unconsciously and
uncritically accepted the inherited patterns of life and
thought that have brought about our present distress.
"We have left undone those things we ought to have
done," he says. Furthermore, because of the urgent need
to make up for past discrimination, he explains that there
must be "education of all white business leaders to the
necessity of asking themselves *every* time an opening or
opportunity occurs, whether a black man can and should
be selected to fill it." Bill Sayre recently wrote to me:
"At the heart of the problem is white feeling, white reaction, white power, white stubbornness, white oppression . . . this on the whites' part, is sin. Sell that, brother,
and the problems are *half* solved." More important than
what he writes is that Bill Sayre acts on whatever he sincerely believes. We must quickly develop legions more
like him, if our nation is to have peace.

Bishop Philip McNairy of the Diocese of Minnesota
spoke of his endorsement of a particular gifted black man
for work in an all-white situation. "I recognize that the
black community needs its own best leaders, especially at
this critical time," he said. "But white people, in a somewhat selfish and perhaps more important way, need to
take whatever reasonable opportunity they can to over-

come their past patterns of exclusion which make them less than what they should be."

All of our institutions need to work in this same spirit.

8. *Work through churches and other organizations to help fellow whites understand that it is in the interests of all that all of our society be desegregated. All men are threatened when the dignity of any man is lessened.*

James Farmer, in pointing out the crucial—and far too long overlooked—difference between integration and desegregation quoted actor and football star Jimmy Brown as saying: "To hell with integration. But, man, don't segregate me." It should be clear that some forms of artificial integration are as degrading as is artificial segregation. People should have the freedom, enforced by law, to make reasonable personal decisions on where they will live and to what extent they will enjoy the benefits of our common life.

"We have to rethink so many things," said Senator Richard Newhouse, Jr., delegate to the Illinois legislature from Chicago's South Side. "So many of our problems simply can't be solved because they haven't been thought through properly. Black people, for one, must learn that there is nothing contrary to integration by their seeking to develop black dignity and group purpose."

Human dignity for all will help to achieve the good life for all. Self-hating people who feel that America is not fully theirs to enjoy are a continuing liability and a drain upon the nation's resources. Men who work to make men's lives better are creators. Men who work, either consciously or unconsciously, to restrict the lives of others thus diminish themselves as well. White churchmen must recognize that they always have the option of noncooperation. If "believing" white people simply did not coop-

erate with those who do not believe in and who work to
destroy the American dream, the course of events would
change overnight. Pious protestations are never a match
for continual deeds. The odds for survival are increasingly against those who fail to act for human dignity for
all. "I ain't nothing," says a disillusioned black youth in
Brooklyn, "and I ain't got nothing to lose if I get killed
burning this *damnation* down."

A friend of mine, much of whose magnificence is in his
stubbornness, takes a delight in quoting Bonaro Over-
street's poem entitled "To One Who Doubts the Wisdom
of Doing Anything If He Can't Do Everything":

> You say the little efforts that I make
> Will do no good?
> To tip the hovering scale
> Where justice hangs in balance?
> > I do not think
> I ever thought they would,
> But I am prejudiced beyond debate
> In favor of my right to choose which side
> Shall feel the stubborn ounces of my weight!

Our country needs to reaffirm this courageous type of
rugged Americanism, stubbornly revealing a determination to make America become, as never before, "the land
of the free and the home of the brave." Each one of us
who has a concern for our urban peace must do no less
than stand firm for the principles for which our nation
ideally stands.

> 9. *Try to eliminate the degrading welfare system
> as we know it today. All men should have some kind
> of responsibility—even it if is clearly "make-work"—
> before they receive any money. Earning for self spells
> dignity. Every man should be allowed this path to*

dignity. Only the completely disabled should be given assistance without a large measure of concomitant responsibility.

The purpose of life is not simply to exist. It is to find fulfillment both for its own sake and in order to enrich the common good. This purpose should be borne in mind, especially as we approach the day of advanced automation, as we shall see in our concluding chapter. We need new definitions of work and leisure. We should bear in mind always that every human being has been endowed with basic talents. They must be identified, developed, and used as fully as possible for the good of our world.

A system based on furthering "the public welfare" should be designed to dignify life and to make possible self-directed growth into self-sufficiency for its citizens. Any welfare system designed to provide long-term relief does not truly serve either the personal or the public good. Until we can change our present system of so-called "welfare," however, we must at least temporarily improve its operation in order to eliminate flagrant practices that lower the dignity of those whom the system is designed to serve.

The growing number of welfare unions must be recognized as serving the urgent purpose of halting, in our publicly sponsored endeavors, the drain on the self-respect of masses of our fellow Americans. Ultimately, the welfare system as we know it should be replaced by a system of human rehabilitation. In my *Black Power and Urban Unrest* (1967) I offered specific suggestions for dealing with this task. Work in this direction must now begin. In every community, committees can be set up now to see how local, state, and national administration of the self-defeating welfare system may be temporarily made more humane. At the same time, the rehabilitation endeavors that must be substituted for the welfare system should be

planned and initiated. Those citizens professionally most
responsible for this area should begin to discover and implement ways to phase out our present welfare system
and to substitute for it a Federally financed program for
human rehabilitation to serve all who need it. A clue to
the type of approach which we should make for substantial changes in the welfare system is inherent in the term
"black power." The concept raises the need for promoting
self-awareness and self-directed growth into self-sufficiency and self-respect. (See discussion in Chapter 9.)

10. *Establish urban planning departments that in-*
clude competent "people-oriented" whites and blacks.

It cannot be said too often that "cities are people."
When we plan for urban needs, we are planning for
people's needs. *And today urban planning is most im-*
mediately necessary for the black community. Yet so far
our planning agencies have not been "people-oriented."
Black planners must be included in top leadership roles,
and all programs must make use of the combined perspectives of at least the disciplines of education, sociology,
social group work, economics, physical planning, and
design. Our philosophers, historians, and theologians also
must contribute their insights to ensure that humanitarian
values are recognized and that the tragic mistakes of
history are not repeated.

The human needs of all are best represented in our day
in the most obvious needs of black people. If we wish to
plan for what our cities need, then we should plan for the
needs of our black communities. The most obviously missing tool in all our planning for urban needs should have
been perceived—at least by the black community—long
ago. Black people have long been aware that they do not
so much have many *basic* problems as they have *one*
basic problem, that is, their oppression as black people.

Some mechanism should be created in every metropolitan area in the nation to make a total assault on that one basic problem.

No competent businessman would think of making a major financial investment in any enterprise without first examining his priorities. Yet, in our dealings with black people's supposed "needs," how are the priorities determined? With whom do we deal? With Joe Blow? With Susie Jones? Or with Mr. Big? Business, civic, and religious leaders who wish to help the black community help itself should always take the most reasonable "first step first" to see that what they propose to do actually represents a priority in terms of the basic needs that black people share.

Only by developing the broadest-based black-leadership coalitions in every metropolitan area in the nation, *including key people from every segment of the black community,* can "local" issues that affect the entire black community be seen in terms of over-all priorities. Past failures to develop such broad-based leadership coalitions account for most of our inability to plan effectively for the most pressing human problems in our urban areas.

The development of such broad-based and inclusive black-leadership coalitions can be made possible only by initial funding from the white community. Such an investment for the basic benefit of a county-wide or metropolitan area would be far more modest than that required by many present programs that benefit only a few. It would most likely cost far less for a metropolitan area than the staffing of almost any traditional neighborhood organization. In later discussion of what black people must do for themselves, we shall describe operating details of such urgently needed coalitions. It should suffice here to say that no funding of *specific projects* should be made for any part of the black community until it is ascertained that they represent actual priorities set by the

larger black community, whose common fortunes are inevitably involved in every such decision. It is basic to
sound planning for urban progress that the required tools
be provided. The encouragement of broad-based metropolitan-area black-leadership coalitions, already long
overdue, should be the first purpose to which the white
community's finances for urban regeneration are addressed.

> 11. *Rethink job-training and hiring policies in in-
> dustry, business, and government. Our education
> system has failed many of our adults, and these
> agencies must take up the slack until necessary edu-
> cational reforms are made. A completely new system
> of "community colleges" could be established for re-
> education of all adults who want it whether or not
> they even finished primary school.*

In his January 23, 1967, address, "Industry—The Responsible Citizen," delivered before the Fifth Annual
Conference of "Plans for Progress," Mr. Donald M. Kendall, President of Pepsi Cola Inc., said to his fellow businessmen:

> Long ago, the old world recognized that the richest
> prospect of the United States was not its unlimited
> natural resources. As early as the eighteenth century
> the influential French economist, De Tocqueville,
> noted that the true richness of the United States was
> the diversity of her various peoples. He said the test
> of America as a nation would rest on how well she
> was able to marshall ethnic differences, welding them
> into a unified national purpose.
> I speak from deep personal experience when I tell
> you that in the 110 countries in which my company
> does business, De Tocqueville's thesis is a frequent

topic of discussion. While we may be dominant in industrial development, *many rightfully regard us as underdeveloped in making full use of our people.* Given a world in which there will be increasingly freer international trade, we can no longer afford not to live up to our full promise. The numbers are simply against us.

While 200 million people live in the United States, nearly three billion live in the rest of the world. In the emerging nations of Africa, Asia, Latin America, and the Middle East, most men are black, brown or yellow. Most of them look to this country for leadership in action—as well as words. Can we afford not to deal with these people because of their color or national origin or accent? Can we afford to be rejected by them? Ridiculous!

Growing internationality in expanding world markets is a common objective of progressive corporations. Business must proceed on the assumption that to range the globe for customers advantages both company and country. How well we compete for our share of international business is in no small part affected by our national image abroad.

It is not technical excellence alone that creates receptivity for our products—mutual ideals also open doors. Trade is often a force for freedom. The wider introduction of U.S. goods in satellite areas can lead to a new and more favorable evaluation of our way of life.

Communist propaganda exploits the fact that our minorities do not have equal opportunity; emerging nations regard us with suspicion. Such feelings retard our business growth, have a negative effect on our world position and hence injure our interests.

Since in expanding world trade we serve national as well as commercial goals, it would be unthinkable

for the government to stand idle and allow an uninformed minority to thwart our growth and thus the
policy of the United States. The government has
every right to expect that organized business will
deal adequately with equal employment opportunities. It is my belief that added government involvement in the form of more regulations and legislation
is not necessary.

I recall that our country entered World War II
with wholly inadequately trained manpower. Yet,
within one year, we had so well mobilized our training structure that we were teaching housewives and
farmers how to make complex electronic assemblies
and close-tolerance machines. Aroused to crisis, our
nation moves swiftly and well.

Mr. Kendall's words are compelling. Yet that significant
overall gains have not been made, despite initiatives taken
by the business community, should stimulate us to seek
new ideas. The President's Commission on Civil Disorders highlighted one explanation of our failure: ingrained and unconscious racism that tends, when unrecognized and uncontrolled, to shape even our best-intentioned endeavors. If, as Mr. Kendall points out, we were
able to mobilize our employment machinery for crisis
even with the perspectives of the early 1940s, we should
and can do so today, in a manner consistent with our
present enlarged insights into what our common life
should be.

The needed authentic community-oriented college enterprise of which Ben Wright speaks can supplement the
work of industry and be the most efficient instrument yet
conceived to serve the growing needs of business and
industry while it also serves the nation's broader human
needs. Such an enterprise would take all adults—whatever
their past training—and, using a developmental approach,

coach and teach them in such ways as to provide high-school-equivalency certification at the same time that skills on at least the associate-degree level were being developed. An atmosphere of adult status and reward is essential to the most effective adult education. We shall touch upon this type of enterprise more in Chapter 10. (See also my *Black Power and Urban Unrest*, Chapter 3, for a detailed presentation on this subject.)

12. *Demand that labor unions stop discriminating, that banks alter their lending practices, that stores alter the higher price structures that are sometimes apparent in branches in black communities.*

Recently I spent an evening in the company of a Federal judge. He was intrigued by the idea of building power for our presently powerless black citizens. He spoke of his own endeavors to persuade white leaders to recognize that the sense of powerlessness is like pressure on a powder keg and that increased pressure makes catastrophe certain. The judge is a thoughtful man from whom I have learned much. We need many more like him. He pointed out that right now labor-union discrimination—which is the major ingredient in depriving black people of economic power—could be ended almost overnight by the Federal government. The National Labor Relations Board, without whose services the unions would be impotent, has an anticommunist provision attached to its service. By adopting a "pro-American" provision, demanding that unions represent the interests of all laboring Americans, it could ensure that discrimination would vanish.

White customers can also demand that stores and banks with which they do business do not add to injustice and urban unrest by discriminatory policies.

13. *Facilitate Negro investment in business and especially in housing. People who own something are not prone to destroy it. Any people—if not included equitably in the system—will tend to disrupt and destroy. All that black people want is a ray of hope, some beginning at fulfillment of promises.*

The New York Times of November 17, 1967, carried a large advertisement by the Schickel Environmental Development Company of Ithaca, New York. The advertisement exemplifies what must be acknowledged as fair-minded and creative thinking of the kind that must increasingly characterize the white leadership in both local and national communities:

An Open Letter to President Johnson,
to Each Member of the Congress,
and to the People of the United States

Proposal for a National Act of Restitution: it is now over two hundred years since the Negroes of the United States were brought here in slavery, and while it is over one hundred years since the abolition of slavery, its brand still exists in the minds of both blacks and whites. It is not enough to be told that you are not slaves, or to be told a hundred years later that you are equal to everyone else. Centuries of deprivation are not erased by words or gestures.

Despite the temptation for whites to disclaim any responsibility for what happened in the past, we do not believe that there exists a responsible American who does not feel guilt about the situation. The truth is that, "The sins of the fathers are visited upon the sons," and that like it or not we must cope with the situation left us by our ancestors, or prepare to be guilty of handing down to our children the fruits of our indifference.

The recent civil rights acts and federal programs have been major steps forward: they have also been learning experiences. If they have done anything, they have made us aware of the Negro's very healthy and very American conviction that he does not want things done for him: he does not want to be a welfare case: he wants to use the resources of the United States to help himself. However, in helping himself the Negro faces difficulties that most cannot overcome without assistance.

We propose a National Act of Restitution to the Negro, which would last for twenty-one years and cut across an entire generation. It would be a Negro Bill of Rights patterned after the G.I. Bill of Rights.

The G.I. Bill recognized that, while fighting for freedom, our boys had missed the normal educational opportunities and that their careers had been interrupted. It was a nation's way of making up for the disruption to their lives that the war had caused. Who can calculate the benefits to individuals, families, and to the nation from the act of national generosity and foresight?

The Negro Bill of Rights should be our attempt, however inadequate, to make up for 100 years of educational and economic deprivation, and unequal treatment.

We suggest that such a Bill of Rights might include at least the following:

1. The right to free education. The right to receive this education in any subject from the most simple to the most learned. The right to receive this education in any school for which they can qualify educationally. As under the G.I. Bill, they would be paid while going to school.

2. Free medical and dental care to ensure that physical disabilities do not prevent the fullest achievement.

3. Very low interest (3%), long-term loans, for the purchase of homes and business enterprises to assist the Negro in achieving a proportionate stake in the American economy.

This program would give the Negro an opportunity to help himself. The benefits would be his by right. It would make him an important economic power which businesses would be competing to serve. When the Negro consumer controls resources, and is free to choose where those resources will be spent, economic competition for this market will help eliminate discrimination.

In addition to being a payment on a moral debt to the Negro, the program would be an economic, social, and political benefit to the Nation. It will go a long way toward releasing the energies and talents of more than 10% of our population, thus enriching the whole Nation and also reducing the mounting costs associated with the bad living conditions of much of the Negro population.

Schickel Environmental Development Company
100 Fairview Square
Ithaca, New York

14. *Support all self-help organizations like the Urban League, CORE, N.A.A.C.P., S.C.L.C., S.N.C.C., and others that may be purely local.*

Choose those through whom you would like best to serve by giving your support. Re-examine the reasons for your choices. Such re-examination may serve your own self-awareness.

Present black efforts toward self-help represent a

healthy trend in the nation's life. Throughout the nation there is a fear of crippling taxation. When people remain dependent, they become a drain on our tax resources. Yet it is harder to find funds for efforts at reasonable self-development than for efforts that simply sustain life at a subsistence level. The greatest difficulties that I encounter in my efforts to describe to white people the new trends toward human dignity and freedom are almost invariably among those whose past efforts have been to shelter black people. Sheltering, on one hand, and facilitating growth into self-sufficiency and self-respect, on the other, are two vastly different approaches. All men need temporary shelter. Only a very few need it forever. The sheltering mentality should be checked out in all of us. Then we must control its manifestations in our support of others.

We must, in every way possible, develop a new stance of affording genuine growth-producing help which will lead to self-sufficiency. In Chapter 3 of *Black Power and Urban Unrest*, I have dealt in detail with the difference between the philosophy of *noblesse oblige*, the giving of relief, and the impetus toward rehabilitation. Our support of the local self-help groups which show the most obvious signs of facilitating growth into self-sufficiency must be encouraged at every hand.

15. *Accept your own inadequacies as white people. Only in this way may your own growth into greater self-sufficiency be assured.*

A suburban clergyman recently told how he has helped his frightened white parishioners to face their fears of black rebellion. He was appalled at the number of requests made to him to sign requests for gun permits, especially as there was no evidence whatever that black people were setting out toward white suburbia or were killing white people. On the contrary, the opposite was true. He explained that many of his people equated black distress with the need for higher taxes, and this prospect they could not face. Already overmortgaged, overtaxed, and financially overextended in many other ways, these people saw every sign of urban unrest as an immediate threat to their precarious way of life. "Many of our people," he says, "are now coming to the realization that they should at least use the urban unrest as a means of helping the country as a whole create more equitable taxation where those in the middle are not caught forever in their presently crippling bind." Furthermore, it must be understood that white fears that black people are going to "come and get them"—which prompts many whites to arm for the further massacre of black people—are largely projective. White people should recognize their reactions for what they are and should deal with their fears in far more creative ways. Dr. Alvin Poussaint of the Department of Psychiatry at Tufts University Medical School explains that the psychotic needs of the American white man in the late 1800s and early 1900s prompted him to project onto the black man his own "violence to murder, ravaging sexual impulses, etc." Dr. Poussaint writes, "The intensity of the white man's psychological need that the Negro be shaped in the image of this projected mental sickness was such as to inspire the whole system of organized discrimination, segregation and exclusion of Negroes from society."

Black people, in their rejection of the results of white psychosis, are effecting a cure, which will ultimately benefit the white men, of a long-standing hereditary disease. White leaders must take far greater initiative in explaining to whites their behavior for what it truly is. In this way, the inappropriate reaction mislabeled "backlash" will not continue to divide and confuse our society.

16. *Organize white leadership to respond to and*

encourage the new mood of self-awareness and self-respect among the leadership of the black community and to combat rampant racism in the white community.

Sympathetic white people, whose voices have not been raised in concerted strength for sanity and decency, should organize themselves to deal with those things that are their unique task. Black leadership that offers new and reasonable insight should receive collective white support. And racism within the white community can best be dealt with by white people in an organized way.

Most often, when white people ask black people what they can or should do to help, the best answer is simply to spread clarifications and principles among their fellows. In the final analysis, each person must come to grips each day with changing situations in his own circle of relationships. Pat answers may illustrate principle, but they can never provide adequate solutions to live issues that change from day to day.

White people can and should get together in their own community, business, and other relationships and continually think through and subscribe to thoughtful combined approaches that may promise more success than those adopted in the past.

17. *Reflect on your own personal part in continuing the white culture patterns on political, social, and economic bases.*

Mrs. Arnita Young Boswell of The University of Chicago School of Social Work, sister of Whitney Young, raises helpful questions about the role of the white family in fostering our culture patterns. "A primary function of family life," she points out, "is to prepare people to be accepting of others." The white family shows greater tendencies toward rejection of those outside its circle than does the black family. "Perhaps it would be to our advantage," Mrs. Boswell suggests, "to give far greater weight than we have done in the past to a re-examination of white family life."

A group of white women was present when a national church executive launched a verbal attack on Lee Montgomery of Temple University for trying to share fresh insights on the education of black urban youth that he had gained from his unusual experiences in Philadelphia. "He didn't hear you at all," said one of the women. "I feel so ashamed," she added, "that we have made our white men feel so much like they are kings that they cannot tolerate the idea that others have anything new or creative to say." Her judgment was a harsh one, in which, to my surprise, the other women present agreed.

That something has gone wrong is certain. New clues must be sought, examined, and dealt with on their merits. The white community has far to go, as is suggested in the following letter from William K. Fox to the leaders of a local Volunteers for McCarthy committee:

Dear Co-workers:

Please inform the "Volunteers for McCarthy" workers of my resignation from the Steering Committee. This is an action I have taken after attending a couple of meetings, reading some of the promotional materials, and rethinking my own position.

I stand with you one hundred percent on the Peace Issue. However, my major concern is the promotion of the interests of the Black Community so that the greatest good may be realized by all. It is the latter interest that I do not see as very much of a concern by the presently composed "Steering Committee"— well-meaning and devoted as I am certain it is.

My real value to the movement would be to relate

selected leadership within the Black Community to the effort; this in itself would be a herculean task. However, if there is also the problem of dealing with a mind-set and cultural background which really has no sympathy or understanding of the importance of this, it would require more of me and people like me than I can afford to give at this time.

My time is too valuable and scarce to use in this way. I prefer to use it with my own group in a gigantic struggle to put us in a position of political power where we can really do the total community and the nation some good. I am sure that there will be other times along the way that we can work together. However, I prefer to do my "missionary work" through the Church and hard political work on an entirely different basis.

I think I know of your personal interest in what I am saying and wish you the best of luck in your efforts.

Sincerely,
W. K. FOX,
President, Tri-Citizens
Economic Union, Inc.

Bill Fox thought that perhaps his letter might be of some small help in sounding the alarm for well-intentioned white people to face their own culturally conditioned patterns. White people must address themselves, undoubtedly with the help of black people, to a rediscovery of what "makes them tick."

18. *Do your part to help America grow into maturity for the sake of its own internal peace and the greater good that this nation can and must represent to the world.*

The much-discussed incident at the White House, in which Miss Eartha Kitt spoke up in a manner allegedly lacking in social grace but bursting with a deep sense of social responsibility, reflected much of the immaturity in our national character. There are those who believe—and I am among them—that the basic blame for much of our national weakness, or pathology, must be placed upon black people for their past failure, understandable as it may be, to enter fully into the power dynamics of the nation's life. Nonetheless, the apparent preference, among those who criticized Miss Kitt, for "polished evasion" over "rough and ready truth" suggests our national immaturity. This failure must be faced and dealt with primarily by responsible leaders in our white communities.

The recent emotion-laden denial of his congressional seat to the Reverend Adam Clayton Powell may also be seen as a case in point. Whatever we may feel about Adam Powell as a man, the attack upon him—and his arbitrary treatment—arose from the immaturity of white people and their inability to accept black people. "Mr. Powell's great mistake," says one white leader, "was to assume that we white people had grown up."

Black Americans, in their reactions to the Powell affair, were nearly unanimous on two counts. They have long shared mixed feelings of disapproval and delight at Mr. Powell's arrogant emulation and exposure of white immorality. Black Americans were of nearly one mind also in their disapproval of *the method* by which Mr. Powell was brought to supposed justice. Black Americans were largely alone in protesting against the manner in the exceptional handling of Mr. Powell *before* he was barred from his seat. Afterward, a substantial white protest against the obvious injustice was raised. Distinguished senators, including Robert Kennedy of New York, and distinguished church bodies and churchmen, notably the New Jersey State Council of Churches, the Presbytery of New York, and the Episcopal bishops of Newark, expressed belated white concern at the peculiar *manner* of dispensing "justice" in Mr. Powell's case.

Both the Presbytery of New York and the New Jersey State Council of Churches described Mr. Powell as a particularly useful public servant and questioned the unique deviation from customary due process and tradition in the manner of his removal from his committee chairmanship and from his seat, even though only temporary. Ben Anderson, the editor and publisher of the *Westchester Observer* of Mt. Vernon, New York, in a poem entitled "Adam You Forgot," underscores the prevailing American failure to deal fairly and maturely with black people:

> We didn't want to do it, Adam.
> We knew it wasn't right.
> But, we just had to show you Adam.
> Adam, you ain't white.
> We know that we've done worse.
> Since Congress first began.
> But, you forgetting Adam.
> You're a colored man.
> When it came to performance,
> You really were an ace.
> But, you forgot yourself.
> You forgot your place.
> We had to show you, Adam,
> To remind you of the fact
> That, whatever else you are,
> Adam, you are black.
> We didn't want to do it, Adam.
> We know that it was wrong.
> But, Adam, you forgot
> Where colored folk belong.

It is a harsh truth from which we cannot escape that both children and uncivilized men act from caprice, whereas civilized adults govern themselves by law.

19. *Seek opportunities to fulfill your best hopes and to preserve your best principles.*

We cannot afford, in the face of our present peril, to let our fear of the new stand in the way of our better judgment. We must always be open to new truths and new awareness.

It was exhilarating to witness recently the reactions of a group of more than 100 high-school teachers to explanation of some implications for classroom teachers drawn from reports on civil disorders. "Whew!" exclaimed one older teacher. "We appreciate this help so much. I personally feel relieved on the one hand, that is, freed from so many frustrating conceptions of the past. But I am burdened with new responsibilities on the other hand." Another teacher arose and said: "What we now need is some steady help in translating what we have heard into some practical guidelines which can serve our needs from day to day. I think that, with such help, we here at our school can work out these guidelines for ourselves and for the benefit of other teachers elsewhere."

Only as white people are willing to develop far more enthusiasm for such rare "listening and heeding" than they have shown in the past are we going to be able to outgrow our present distress. White people must make some major adjustments in their relationships with black people and in their approaches to black people's needs. The Ford Foundation and the Urban Coalition—along with other agencies of business, government, and philanthropy —should seek leadership and advice from elements in the black community that represent the new mood of self-

awareness. New black insights and abilities are ingredients
essential to the solution of our urban distress.

E. Douglas White of the Detroit Industrial Mission
wrote to me on May 2, 1968, as follows:

> I am writing to thank you for the assistance which
> you offered us in our efforts to secure an additional
> member for the staff of the Detroit Industrial Mission.
> . . . I think our efforts have probably given us two ob-
> ject lessons. The first is the explosion of the myth
> about the lack of so-called "qualified Negroes." It's
> our conviction that a quantitative assessment of
> available people is a direct function of the quality of
> commitment one brings to the task of recruiting. The
> second object lesson is that any organization which
> does not actively seek the resources available to it
> from the black community in the form of personnel
> and consultative relationships is missing out on an
> opportunity to avail itself of the most relevant and
> critical resources in society today.

We can, if we but will to do so, always find opportunities to fulfill our best hopes—and we may do so to our
profit!

*20. Compensate for abuses that our historically
white-controlled and white-defined society has created, in every enterprise in which we are engaged.*

Provide bail and appeal money, whenever possible, for
those who are unduly harassed by the faulty justice that is
almost inevitable for black people. In almost every city in
the nation free or low-cost legal advice and bail should be
provided or extended to produce an immediate semblance
of justice. In many cities it costs harassed black litigants

two to three times more to achieve justice than it costs
white people, as the former are most often prejudged
guilty in the lower courts. While such funds and services
are being set up, responsible white citizens will also set
about the business of reforming the functioning of the
bench and officers of the peace, reforms that will benefit all.

Declare moratoria in employment and personnel advancement until black people are afforded equity. Mere
"equal" opportunity, even if sincerely offered, will never
bring genuine equality now. At best it will only keep
inequality from growing broader. In every firm, agency
and institution in the land, black people have been arbitrarily denied opportunity to some degree. This denial
has increased each white person's opportunity and
brought the risk of massive and sustained black rebellion
closer. We must provide *greater*-than-equal opportunity
to all black people, chiefly through re-evaluating the skills
of those presently employed. White employers—whose
skill at problem solving is one of the wonders of the
world—add to social costs each time they fail to solve
the "problem" of equitable employment for black people.
"Where there is a will there is a way," but we still have
not found a way of closing the opportunity gap between
white and black Americans. In Newark, New Jersey, as
in many other cities, unskilled white laborers are im-
ported, and still industry cries that black people do not
have sufficient skills for employment.

Be honest in your planning for educational and other
benefits for black people. In Essex County, New Jersey,
a county college was opened in the express hope that it
would fit the educational needs of black youth. Few black
students applied, as the standards for admission were
largely applicable to the needs of white young people.
If we are genuinely concerned about meeting the needs

of black people—and also about the hard-core problems of all people in circumstances of greatest economic distress—then those trained people who are most sensitive to these needs should *plan and direct* our solutions. Otherwise, we shall continue merely to go through the motions, to satisfy our consciences that we are "doing something," while white planners and technicians are rewarded financially and the urgent circumstances of black people grow progressively worse.

America in many ways owes a debt to black people. Black people have served the needs of the nation without receiving their just rewards. They have been denied their rights and their share in the benefits due to all who are part of the nation. Our racist culture has deprived black people of dignity; our institutions have crippled them by offering a future variously labeled "frustration," "rejection," "bitterness," "emptiness," and "despair." And all this denial has occurred in an atmosphere of innocence and self-righteousness.

"In such measure as you give," it has been said, "so shall you be given." Small wonder, then, that guilt at the growing unrest in our cities is rising among white Americans nurtured on the Scriptures. Yet cosmic justice is tempered always by mercy. The clear need is for white men to "cease and desist" in their thwarting of human fulfillment. White men who are themselves just will work thoughtfully and aggressively to re-establish the justice that human fulfillment for all requires.

For the benighted and the abused, however, there is always at hand some effective means for achievement of—and helping others to achieve—self-fulfillment. Throughout history, majorities have never been able in periods of great crisis, on their own, to save themselves. They have required the initiative of minorities. So it may be in our present time of peril. We have dealt with what

white people in America *can* do. We now turn to what
black people *must* do to save both themselves and the
nation, which must be designed for the full enjoyment of
all or perhaps cease providing for the enjoyment of any.

CHAPTER SIX

Knowing the Beauty
of What We Are

ONE OF MY MOST UNFORGETTABLE EXPERIENCES AS A YOUNG altar boy at St. Andrew's Church in Cincinnati occurred after the 11:00 service one Sunday morning. It was Father Oxley's custom to greet his parishioners and visitors at the main door of the church as they left. The altar boys took turns making themselves handy near the door.

On this particular Sunday, a proud-looking white woman had visited the church. Father Oxley, noting her British accent, asked where her home was. "I am visiting here from England," was her pleasant answer. His handsome dark West Indian face came alive with delight. "I am a Britisher, too," he said. "I was born in Trinidad." His affirmation of a kind of patriotic kinship was received with devastating scorn. "You are *not* a Britisher!" the visitor replied with fierce contempt. "You are a British *subject*."

That experience was one of many that drove into my consciousness, during my early years, how low in esteem and power black people are. The abrupt change to brusque unkindliness by one who had only an instant before appeared to be a thoroughly gracious lady, however, gave me particular pause. Just what kind of graciousness could be so deeply lacking in grace? That specific instance of gratuitous belittlement before his parishioners of a man who, in my young eyes, deserved great respect haunted me for years. It brought into focus for me the need for black people to deal far more effectively than we had done before with the issues of group respect and power —and I have wrestled with these issues ever since.

In this chapter, we shall examine some aspects of growing black self-awareness and self-respect. In the next chapter, we shall examine some current promising approaches to the long-standing struggle for black group status and power. In Chapter 8, we shall discuss how the growth of black self-awareness and the development of black group power may serve as vital ingredients in the reordering of our presently fractured national and global society.

It is only one of countless strange occurrences of history that a black man in his mid-twenties, already branded by many as a wild and reckless militant, should raise and bring into focus for the benefit of our nation and the world the two most basic needs in all our personal and community lives: first, the need to come to terms with oneself, to discover the beauty of what one essentially is, and, second, the need for power to fulfill individual promise. Black power—the most creative social concept of the present century—thus is designed only incidentally, although most immediately, to encourage black people to discover their own identities and to create *for themselves* group power. All of us must come to terms with who we are. Some people in the insurance business claim that more than 90 per cent of automobile accidents are related to identity problems. Many social scientists believe that our soaring incidence of mental disease and our mounting divorce and delinquency rates—along with obvious aspects of our foreign relations and other unresolved domestic social problems—also attest to the serious identity crisis that we collectively face.

It is good, then, that black people at least are beginning a process that should be entered upon by the nation as a whole: the sometimes awkward struggle for self-awareness.

"Prunes and Prisms"

My mother was a beautiful woman of golden-brown complexion, and she carried herself with great dignity. Both as a schoolteacher and as a mother she exercised great care of those for whose upbringing she felt responsible. She went to her reward when I was twelve.

I am told that among the Samoans there is a legend about creation that squares with my own early perceptions of reality. The story is that, when God sought to create man in his own image, he first shaped the clay and then baked it. The first clay was a bit too light. He tried again, and the second clay was darker than the ideal. On the third attempt the clay came out a rich golden brown in the exact image of the Creator. He looked upon this precise model of himself and smiled!

Among black people there are all shades; some are light, some are golden brown, and some are deep brown. But my mother's complexion, in my early conception of reality, was perfect, the best that the Creator could give to man or woman.

My twin brother and I are somewhat darker than our parents were. Our two sisters, Lina and Lydia, are quite fair, what was referred to as *marrone*. In our household there were thus all the colors that make up our race. Our parents were eager that we come to see ourselves in a positive way and to accept our heritage as good. Yet somehow I came to feel that, although my mother's rich golden-brown complexion was the most beautiful that God had made, it was still necessary to improve upon His work. Thick lips, for instance, had to be kept pulled in tight lest they appear too large.

Mom, like many other mothers of that period, would have us stand before a mirror and go through the exercise of saying "prunes and prisms" while pulling our lips in gently. Madam A'Lelia Walker, who invented the hot hair-straightening comb, was also a kind of patron saint in our household. Our parents dressed us somewhat lavishly. We were scrubbed and brushed and pressed, and our arms and legs were oiled so that the ashen or rusty look that dark skin often develops in cold weather would take on a satiny luster. We were taught to be proud but also to be as much like the white ideal as our black selves could be. Like so many "refined" white Americans who try to emulate the English, we either could not or would not accept ourselves for what we were. We were not even conscious of our self-depreciation.

The story here is in a sense a tragic one, but it represents a well-nigh universal experience among black people brought up in the United States. At the same time that we have striven for pride in what we have been, what we are, and what we yet may be, we have taken as our unacknowledged but universal model the ideal white American. Ludicrous evidence of this split are the occasional black men who, having spent all their lives in a black American world, speak with a Cockney accent.

We have sought, albeit unconsciously, to be carbon copies of what we could not and should not be in fact. What seems especially unfortunate is that we have sought to purchase stock in a value system that tends—despite its ethical component—to give a higher priority to material things than to human values. We have largely copied rather than creatively adapted these values, often taking form without substance, a tendency that has compounded our tragedy. But it must be made absolutely clear that *our efforts to be like white people, even emulating their disdain for blackness, have, ironically, served our survival.*

Unconscious black self-hatred is the black side of the racism that permeates the nation. It is self-destructive insofar as it works to make black people "acceptable" and worthwhile to the larger society at the price of diminishing black identity, integrity, and self-respect.

The effects of this tragic ambivalence, however, touch the lives of all Americans, for those who will destroy themselves are not meticulous in setting limits on what else they will destroy. Black people, in their perilously benighted condition, cannot afford any longer to seek to be what they are not. Nor can the nation encourage such self-hatred or sit idly by as its corrosive effects day by day endanger the nation's future.

Furthermore, it should be clear to all in the United States today that fulfillment can come to the nation as a whole *only* when it comes to every member of the nation. Black people cannot offer the nation their very best at the same time that they hate themselves and devote their energies to being other than what they are. Self-discovery and self-awareness are necessary gateways to maturity and fulfillment. The immaturity that pervades our nation is of a piece with—and partly rooted in—the failure, however understandable historically, of black America to come into its own.

For this reason, every American should rejoice at what our black young people especially are seeking to do, as they add their concerted efforts to the struggle that generations before them have fought with varying degrees of effectiveness. They are seeking to end the negative aspects of the "prunes and prisms" days and to promote in new ways what is called "black consciousness" and "black pride." They see consciousness of group identity as part of the development of power for black people to relate to others *as they choose* with dignity and command.

These young people recognize the validity of Alexis de Tocqueville's observation that much of the genius of America was that here men with common perceptions of their plight would seek one another out. United this way, they were no longer impotent or isolated men but "a power seen from afar." The perception of our common condition as black people is perhaps the basic ingredient of black consciousness. It is the foundation stone for group power.

Being "For Real"

Black consciousness, as Mrs. Rowena Rand of Washington, D.C., puts it, is essentially the capacity for knowing who and what we are. One proud black lady at an "urban affairs" meeting at Quinnipiac College in Hamden, Connecticut, explained that being black simply means being "for real." Noting that some white people cannot understand black people's "soul talk," the lady explained, "You've got to be 'for real' to read us."

The August 1967 issue of *Redbook* contained an article by Jean Smith, a former S.N.C.C. volunteer with the Mississippi Freedom Democratic Party, now married and living in Greenville, Mississippi. The article was entitled "I Learned to Feel Black." Mrs. Smith's story typifies the spirit of self-discovery, of being "for real," that growing numbers of black young people are experiencing. It is a story worth examining carefully either in *Redbook* or in the excellent collection of basic essays, *The Black Power Revolt*, edited by Floyd B. Barbour. Jean Smith's story is one of rebirth, of growth into a new and liberating self-awareness, which is, after all, the only life pattern that can bring personal and collective fulfillment.

Jean Smith was an idealistic freedom worker in the early 1960s, when to be a member of S.N.C.C. was still regarded by the public generally as representative of American idealism at its best. She writes:

> When I left Washington, D.C. [where she was a student at Howard University], in 1963 to go South with S.N.C.C., you knew me. Now, four years later, I am a different person.
> Essentially the difference is that I became consciously black. I came to understand that there wasn't room enough in the society for the mass of black people, that the majority of Americans are acting either in unbearably bad faith or in tragic ignorance when they project to their children the image of an American society where all men are free and equal. (*The Black Power Revolt*, p. 209)

The bulk of Mrs. Smith's article is a moving recapitulation of her disillusioning experience with the Mississippi Freedom Democratic Party. She speaks of her own stubborn idealism and of her resistance to recognizing that the freedom movement did not and could not, under circumstances prevailing in the black and white communities, win the freedom that it sought. "I had invested so much of myself in the fight," she writes, "that I didn't want to admit that it came to so little."

"The best way to understand," the article continues, "is to look at what the Negro people who cast their lot with the Movement believed." Here is the heart of her presentation:

> The crux of the matter is that they believed that there was a link between representation in government and making that government work for you. What they—and I—discovered was that, for some people,

this link does not exist. For most black people, voting
has not much more benefit than the exercise of walking to the polls. Why is this the case? Because the
link between voting and partaking of the benefits of
society exists at the pleasure of society. The society
must be willing to respond to the legitimate needs of
the people; only then can the channels for the expres-
sion of these needs, such channels as voting, be mean-
ingfully employed.

A dramatic example is glaringly visible today on
the national scene. In January of 1967, when Adam
Clayton Powell was barred from his seat in the House
of Representatives, he was prevented from acting for
his Harlem constituents, the people of the 18th Congressional District of the State of New York, who had
elected him. When he was stripped of his chairmanship of the House Education and Labor Committee,
he was stripped of the power effectively to represent
the Negro people, a power it had taken him 22 years
to build. He was prevented from representing these
people because the majority of Congress, which in
this instance speaks for the larger society, does not
want him. It is as simple as that.

Our effort in the South to enter the society through
the use of the vote came to an anticlimax because we
had been lied to. We had worked feverishly to qualify
under objective standards for our rights, only to learn
that these rights are arbitrarily conferred by those
in power. In the end, we learned that there are a
thousand ways for a people who are weaker than the
rest to be "kept in their place," appeals to good conscience notwithstanding. There are simple mechanisms, like last-minute changes in election laws and
altering the boundaries of election districts. And there
are subtler means, such as making bank loans to the
"leaders" of a poverty-stricken community so that

they can never afford to disagree with you; such as busing newly eligible voters off to Florida to pick fruit. (pp. 211–12)

It was through such experiences that the Jean Smiths— the youthful idealists who had the greatest faith in possibilities for achieving good for all through the existing order of relationships—lost their hope. Or, as Boston's Byron Rushing puts it, they died to their old awarenesses that they might be reborn.

Jean Smith now finds herself with a new orientation, away from excessive or needless dependence among black people and toward both black initiative for the entire nation's good and a new kind of cooperative alliance—based on mutual maturity—with white people. In the remainder of this chapter, we shall examine Jean Smith's seven precepts for black group self-awareness as I have extracted them from her own story. They are representative in a sense of the new synthesis of what black America has sought through the years to achieve.

New Principles

Our young people today are reminding us of precepts that date back among our people to Benjamin Banneker and Henry Garnet and can be traced down through Marcus Garvey and Walter White to the present.

Benjamin Banneker (1731–1806) was an astronomer and surveyor, one of a team of three men who set out the boundaries of Washington, D.C. Banneker, like Henry Garnet, a Presbyterian minister who lived a generation later, was a militant advocate of both black pride and development of black potential for the nation's growth. Marcus Garvey and Walter White were black elder statesmen during my youth. Although each had a unique program, they were united in their conviction that black people must share an awareness of the prophetic role that they can and should play in the world.

1. *Growth comes from within.* The long-standing conviction that only through prior self-development can personal and corporate fulfillment be achieved is restated in Jean Smith's youthful yet wise words. She writes, capturing for today the spirit of our black forebears, as follows:

> Negroes must turn away from the preachings, assertions and principles of the larger society and must turn inward to find the means whereby black people can lead full, meaningful lives. We must become conscious that our blackness calls for another set of principles, principles on whose validity we can depend because they come from our own experiences. (p. 217)

Growth can be stimulated by externals, but it occurs only in accordance with inner needs. By learning who we are and by becoming our best selves we also learn to relate to others. Our purpose is to develop *the capacity* to cooperate or to combine our interests with those of others, whether or not the capacity is used. Maturity is achieved when people are in a position to engage in equitable interrelationships. Our focus then must be upon the use of our own experiences as the foundation for our own growth.

Everyone in America should insist that black people develop themselves to enrich the nation's common life. An African proverb has it that "The day of weaning is the day of birth." We must become ourselves *as black people* before we can hope to relate with integrity to others and so make our unique and invaluable contribution to a good life in which we and all others may share. Indeed, the search for inner resources is part of the universal process of growth that black Americans, in a strategic way, may encourage in all of us.

"Should we not be color blind?" is a question that every black American is asked sooner or later. While recognizing the good will of the questioner, we must answer unequivocally "no!" Not "in spite of our blackness" but "in and through" our own precious—and, for most of us, rediscovered—black integrity we must join equally in a common humanity.

The regenerative possibilities in what Vincent Harding of Atlanta's Spellman College calls "the gift of blackness" must be added to our common values. We shall look at this gift more closely in Chapter 8. It is enough at this point to underscore the fact that black people must temporarily put preponderant emphasis upon the too long neglected task of looking inward. Our immaturity—and the immaturity of the nation as a whole—can be overcome in large measure as we become far more self-aware. This growth involves controlling—or, better, casting off—our unconscious self-hatred and *looking within far more appreciatively*.

2. *Black consciousness does not exclude integration.* It simply does not require integration as an absolute end. Integration (or, more accurately, "desegregation," which subordinates *social* integration) is only a means to achieve freedom and fulfillment for all. Jean Smith writes:

I think the fight for integration must continue because we derive some benefits from it. It means better living conditions for a few of us, a few more yearly incomes above the poverty level. It means that we can feel more like men and women because we've insisted on the rights that society says are ours. (pp. 217–18)

There are only limited dividends from some forms of "integration," not because integration is not good, but partly because, to be effective, it requires equitable power

relations *first*. The staff of the N.A.A.C.P. Legal Defense
Fund thus views black self-awareness as basic to the ac-
complishment of its purpose. Gustav Heningburg of the
Fund staff believes that, although our commitment to
most forms of integration must not slacken, our emphasis
upon black consciousness must greatly increase. "Low
self-esteem and an apologetic view of what we are worth
as black people," he says, "are primary hindrances in what
the Legal Defense Fund of the N.A.A.C.P. seeks to do."

Similarly, H. Naylor Fitzhugh, black vice-president of
Pepsi-Cola, complains that in his work with business and
industrial leaders our own black low estimates of our due
place in America's life are a major cause of the failure of
these leaders to respond. "Black people need to have their
integration into business programmed and spelled out
more clearly, in qualitative and quantitative, step-by-step
terms, with some accompanying time table, if it is to be
meaningful," Fitzhugh explains. "But the problem is," he
continues, "that black people must take more initiative in
this effort. To date, we have not commanded sufficient
resources to begin to do this in a remotely adequate way."
Those of us already in the white business structures must
band and work together more effectively to add our contributions to those of the valiant professional civil rights
leaders—in order to take the initiative in realistic programming for this kind of integration. Perhaps our rather
naïve efforts to become "integrated" at too superficial a
level have impeded such efforts "in the past."

3. *Achievement of black self-awareness can be facilitated by white cooperation.* Jean Smith writes:

> Obviously, we need access to the capital and to the
> intellectual resources of the larger society. We need
> to know how to build lathes and how to market prod-
> ucts. We need to know the ins and outs of prevailing

political forms and to have access to the body of
scientific knowledge. . . . (p. 217)

Black self-awareness involves using white people creatively instead of being misused by white people. An Urban
League executive noted how he had pounded so hard for
years at the doors of white-controlled industry only to
disover that he was "successful" in having the door opened
only sufficiently to fill industry's needs. This limited gain
is typical of the sad experiences of the past—and the
present—for us all. For we have not closed what the National Urban League calls "the unclosing gap" between
white and black Americans.

Jean Smith mentions our need of capital from the larger
society. It has long been recognized that this capital is
ours by right of "equity and restitution," which is what
the black abolitionist David Walker meant when he wrote
in 1829, "America is more our country, than it is the
whites'—we have enriched it with our *blood* and *tears*."
The Ford and Carnegie Foundations—along with other
agencies for urban and educational development—should
place development and research capital in the hands of
black men of competence. Indeed, these foundations, if
they are to achieve their stated purposes of educational
and urban regeneration, should have black men at their
helms. White people should be accepting—as they must
come to do in the future—urgently needed black ideas on
our educational and urban problems.

The black community must come to see that its basic
problem is a communal one. All elements of the black community must work together and develop a common picture
of the *one basic problem* that is associated with their
shared low status as black people. Then leadership representative of the black community as a whole should
command and control the resources necessary to accom-

plish goals determined in shared and responsible assessment.

Our black young people often ask: "Shall I go on to college? Shall I go to a white college or a black one?" All in our society, young and old alike, need the benefits of continuing education. For black people especially it is necessary for survival. In any educational enterprise we must acquire and develop *tools* and be careful not to acquire the *agenda* of those who teach. With this distinction in mind, the most important consideration is that black people, by whatever reasonable means are available, acquire the necessary tools.

Perhaps the greatest cooperative service that white people can render for our mutual benefit would be financial assistance of thoughtful black people—from all walks of life—who seek to develop new educational models and new prescriptions for urban rehabilitation. White technicians have failed partly because they are equipped only to execute what the architects design, and so far the right architects have not had the opportunity to design.

Self-Development

Black self-awareness involves not only new relationships with white people but also new dedication to the long-neglected task of self-development.

4. *Only on the basis of black group purpose or black consciousness can black institutional life be built.* Jean Smith puts it this way:

We have to build a broad-based black consciousness so that we can begin to depend on one another for economic, political and social support. We have to build our own businesses to put money into the

development of the Negro community, businesses to
establish foundations to support our own new educational and social ventures. We have to make our
politicians more responsible to us so that either they
improve our communities or they go. Living, growing communities must be built to replace our strife-
ridden ghettos. The problems of illiteracy and the
inability to communicate must be tackled. (p. 217)

In August 1967 I had one of the richest experiences of
my life. It was the opportunity to meet the Messenger, the
Honorable Elijah Muhammad. My host in Chicago on
that particular visit was William Meyers, Vice-President
of the Combined Insurance Company of America. Mr.
Muhammad learned that I was in his city and invited me
to tea. He also graciously welcomed my white host, of
whose responsibility for my visit to Chicago he was in-
formed, and for approximately an hour the Messenger
shared something of the richness of his thoughts and emo-
tions with us. I have never heard expressed more beauti-
fully the need for black people to know the innate and
unrealized beauty of their being and to discover the price-
less benefits of simply becoming what they are designed
or "called" to be. In essence, here is what the Messenger
said to us:

We must be self-reliant. Those who are beggars
will forever be treated with disrespect.
Development cannot be an individual enterprise. It
must be shared by those who share our condition of
common oppression.
Black people must know that they are a peculiar
people, in the Old Testament sense, set in the world
to share in its redemption. [This role is, in fact, the
historical role of oppressed minorities. One has only

to read Arnold Toynbee, Martin Luther King, W. E. B.
Du Bois, Pitirim Sorokin, Reinhold Niebuhr, Frantz
Fanon, and Paul Tillich in this regard.]

All people must own and control land to have identity. The earth is a source and symbol of one's past,
present, and future destiny.

Personal pride is a product of group pride. We
must develop group pride. We must be proud of
ourselves as a race. If we are not for ourselves, who
then can—or even should—be for us?

We must never waste our precious energy hating
others. We must show our care for human life by our
willingness to defend it.

A world where violence and the denial of human
values is affirmed must be regenerated by the initiative of black men who know more than do any others
the self-defeating nature of such a world.

We must, in every way possible, set new standards
of justice, beauty, and truth.

Black men must learn that a basic purpose of life
is to cooperate freely with our family first and then
with all others.

As we as black people change, so will our world.

In all my life, I never expected to have a direct confrontation with such an oracle. But I found myself that
day sitting before a prophet who uttered the clear and
simple truths needed for our redemption. Can we afford,
good brothers, to miss his saving message? If the whirl-
wind and the fire spoke divine truth in the days of old,
can we deny the mysteries of truth's operation in our day
where new truth somehow must be proclaimed—and
heard?

5. *Power is needed to deal with others with dignity and
effectiveness.* Jean Smith writes:

Our immediate objective must be the strengthening of the black community instead of the apparently unattainable goal of diffusion of all black people into the main stream of American life. We have to become so strong that we can depend on one another to meet our needs and so that we'll be able to deal with white people as we choose to, not as we are obliged to. (p. 217)

Why have our Jewish brothers been able to survive and to act as creatively as they have done in every society of which they have been a part? Because, first of all, they have been deeply aware of themselves as a people and a worthy people. Maulana Ron Karenga, whom some theologians have called "the nation's new systematic theologian," remarks that the Jews have integrated several key ingredients of their culture in a way that few other groups have done. Black people, he argues, must seek to integrate (and to develop) all the elements that constitute a culture. He lists "the seven criteria for culture":

> mythology
> history
> social organization
> political organization
> economic organization
> creative motif
> ethos

The key is "integration," the integration of all that we as a people are. It should serve as a more than ample basis for our future survival and self-fulfillment.

Moving Ahead

Recently, I had the opportunity to review a mass of literature selected at random from the young so-called "black pride" and "black power" advocates. I must admit that even I was surprised at what I read. Like most black people in America, I tended to believe that a significant number of the new generation wanted out of the American enterprise altogether, although I thought the number was probably exaggerated. I found, however, scarcely a trace of this attitude, even among avowed Marxist thinkers. What I read was a composite manifesto, calling upon black people to cease trying to adopt strange and unproductive ways and to begin to shape the future in ways that are appropriate to their own needs. What I read might best be summed up in the next precept for self-awareness.

6. *Black consciousness is at present the best contribution to the whole country's growth into maturity.* According to Jean Smith:

> I think that after the black community has become strong enough, the rules of the game will change; society may decide to join hands with us on equal terms. It may even decide to join hands with us to build a country where all of us, white and black, can live. (p. 218)

Recently I met at breakfast in Washington, D.C., with a group of undersecretaries from several Cabinet departments and the chief administrators of approximately a dozen Federal agencies. They had read my books and wanted to hear more about the necessity for new definitions of practically all problems relating to black people if we are to have tangible results from our efforts to solve them. One of those present asked me to define the difference between myself and other black leaders. It gave me the opportunity to say what I have learned and what all of us must join in saying: that all black brothers working for freedom mutually reinforce one another. Just as Malcolm X made the N.A.A.C.P. and the Urban League seem "more respectable" and paved the way for Dr. King's international acclaim, any one of us who is "heard" today owes a debt to those who have provided the bafflement that enables us to speak up to clarify and help others to "understand."

Brothers, black brothers everywhere, our freedom and the nation's growth depend upon our development as a group into a kind of maturity based upon self-awareness and upon working together in unity. Even now, we may begin to be heard—and possibly even heeded—if we are conscious of our common condition and our common need for growth for our own and the nation's larger good.

Moving out of old ways is never easy, for change inevitably brings uncertainty. Yet change we must. The younger generation, which is redefining freedom on the basis of historical and immediate black experience, is deeply aware of this fact. This awareness is apparent in the last of the seven precepts that I have extracted from Jean Smith's autobiographical sketch.

7. *Change from old ways is painful but nonetheless good for all.* Mrs. Smith writes:

The call for black consciousness is at first painfully hard to answer. It's hard to start all over again and establish new principles and modes of operation. For we have struggled vainly for so long, trying to approximate white culture! Our artists, our scientists, our leaders, have been respected by us only after they have been "legitimized" by the white world. . . . We face a prodigious task. We've danced to the tune

so long; and now it becomes necessary to stop and
gather our senses, to stop and listen to the tune and
decide which of its elements warrant our response.
(p. 218)

Not long ago I had lunch with one of the eminent black
scientists of the world. He was "open" to the concept of
black power and to the need for black group awareness. I
suggested to him that more than openness was needed.
The younger generation has issued a call. It is up to those
of us with ears to hear, eyes to see, lips to speak, and
hearts and hands to work to respond to this call and to
strive in unity to reveal the good in our common black
heritage. He seemed unmoved. I hope that he was not.

Omar Abu Ahmed serves along with C. Sumner Stone,
Isaiah Robinson, Maulana Karenga, and me as members
of the Committee on Continuation for the 1968 National
Conference on Black Power. Omar Ahmed, a second-gen-
eration Muslim, has perhaps more than any other individual impressed upon me the need for developing—for
the benefit of the entire world—new modes of operational
harmony. We need not be in agreement on many specific
issues as long as we work harmoniously for what we recognize as our common good. First, however, *we must be
aware that we have a deeply urgent common need.* When
we have this awareness we shall have taken the first important step in developing *black* awareness.

It's exhilarating to know—or to rediscover—just who
and what you are. It was good to hear Bishop John Bright
tell his people in Bermuda several years ago that the
future would belong to them if they fulfilled their unique
destiny as black people. The people had sung the stirring
African Methodist Episcopal hymn, "The Church Is Moving On." Bishop Bright told his people to continue the
great tradition of the pioneers of African Methodism, to

set their own priorities, to do their own thinking, and to become leaders of a new world and not followers in a world destined to decay and pass away. There is a scripture verse of which I was reminded by his words; it calls forth some of the beauty that is our heritage as black people. It speaks to us as in a parable.

How beautiful upon the mountains are the feet of him who brings good tidings, who proclaims peace. . . .
Your watchmen shall lift up their voices; with one voice they shall rejoice; they shall see eye to eye, when the great day comes at last!

Shortly before Freida de Knight, food and fashion editor for *Ebony,* died, I suggested to her that she set a new tone for the food and fashion world by emphasizing African motifs and African-made materials. She was open to the idea, and some small but significant beginnings have since been made by Mrs. John Johnson. On every hand, we must become contributors and leaders and pace setters rather than the passive recipients and followers of others' cultures and customs.

There was a moment of reawakening in our own household when we were offered some reproductions of famous works of art and could not decide easily upon using them. Our oldest daughter Lydia, founding president of the Black Students Association at Upsala College, settled the matter by suggesting the obvious. "The most beautiful thing that we could do to brighten our house would be to do something a bit different, which we have already begun to do." Her mother inquired just what that might be. Lydia said: "We can enlarge our black art collection. We already have African carvings. We can add some black American and black African paintings." We are in the process of doing so, beginning with a cultural motif executed by our son Nathan III, who is an art student in New York City.

More and more each day, I find now a wonderful time to be alive, as I see black people being turned on and turning others on. Victor Solomon of Harlem CORE and Preston Wilcox of I.S. 202 in Harlem are typical heralds of a wonderful new day. I spent a morning with them recently at a meeting held, under the leadership of Harry Bright and Dr. Oscar Lee, by the National Conference of Christians and Jews; it was entitled "Black Power: A Positive Force." They underscored for me and for many others who were present that the beauty of realized and integrated black experience may serve the entire nation's good. But first we must begin to become self-aware.

Whenever I see a black youngster—or a black man or woman—with a "natural" hairdo, I recognize that he or she is seeking greater self-awareness. Whatever the path, we must all keep in mind that the end is necessary and glorious. It means that black people are coming to recognize that, as with all men, if they are to be their best, they must be truly themselves.

Black Is Glorious

Rosaline Harris from Pennsylvania wrote "The Retarded Tree" at the age of sixteen:

> They planted in my mind the seed of despair
> They told me my Black face was ugly and so was my
>   kinky hair
> They said no matter how hard I tried, I'd be a slave
>   until I died
> But I was determined to be free

To have my taste of liberty
So I followed them up the down stairs
Bleached my skin and straightened my hair
They said I was dumb and needed an education, so I
     tried that too
Later I found I had been a Black Princess in a white
     man's zoo
All of my life I pursued untruth
Following after the white man with futile proof of his
     . . . truths
Now I'm old, my children are grown
Possessing sweet dreams of their own
They have gone a little further than I
Talking about something called Black pride
They say Black skin is beautiful and so is kinky hair
They say trying to be white just ain't gettin' nowhere
I am old but I know that pride is "our" need
For they have planted in our mind the "retarded
     seed," of "despair-ity"

Barbara Buckner Wright, our second daughter, wrote
the following poem, which is entitled "Black," in 1967,
when she was seventeen:

I am a Negro———
     And I am ashamed.
Chemicals in my hair to make it other than what it is,
Bleaches on my skin to make it more . . . non-black,
Cosmetics on my face to be like the "other"
Why must I try to be other than what I am?

The French say they are French,
               from France,
The Irish say they are Irish,
               from Ireland,

The Italians say they are Italian,
                          from Italy,
And I say I am Negro———
                          from where?

Is there a Negro land?
The French, Irish, Italians all have a culture and
          heritage.
What is My land? Where are My people? My Cul-
          ture? My heritage?
I am a Negro———
          And I am ashamed.
Who GAVE me this name?
"Slaves and dogs are named by their masters ... Free
          men name themselves"*
Must I be other than what I am?

I am Black. This is a source of pride.
My hair is short and finely curled.
My skin is deep-hued, from brown to black.
My eyes are large, open to the world.
My lips are thick, giving resonance to my words.
My nose is broad to breathe freely the air.
My heritage is my experience *in* America ... although
          not *of* it;
Free from pretense; open to truth
Seeking freedom that all life may be free

I am Black. America has cause to be proud.

Arthur Earley writes of the new spirit abroad among
our black young people. He admonishes those of us who
are older to heed their words of warning and supplication.
He reports, "The most spectacular phenomenon extant in
Black America today is the enthusiastic and inspiring preoccupation of our black youth with the development of

* Maulana Ron Karenga in *The Quotable Karenga* (1967)

black pride and self-determination among the black community."

In his position paper in "The Emerging Black Community," prepared for a retreat at Radnor, Pennsylvania, in January 1968, Mr. Earley lamented that so many older people, both black and white, are separated from young people by a "generation gap." This gap, he believes, must be closed. The burden rests chiefly upon the older and ostensibly more sober and reflective adults to bridge the gap of suspicion, distrust, and misunderstanding. This effort is of the greatest urgency, for in fact "the future of Black America is in the hands of our black youth."

To those who sometimes criticize our youth for not having a positive program, Arthur Earley replies on two levels. He believes, first, that young people are saying a number of positive things and, second, that they are asking for help from all others in the black community, working together. In fact, the latter point represents a new stance, seeking a broad response in terms of self-development and self-determination from the entire black community. It is not the traditional appeal for a chiefly personal response or one from a few appointed leaders who may then speak to the consciences of white people. New words, even if they fulfill in a glorious way old desires, are sometimes painful to hear. Our young people therefore must add a thoughtful and appreciative patience to their firm and unwavering insistence that "new occasions teach new duties."

Mr. Earley describes the positive message that black youth, using its own language forms, is attempting to communicate to us all:

An examination of the slogans of our black youth will, if understood, reveal a blueprint by which the entire black community could be melded into the most powerful ethnic group in America; to wit:

"*Black Power*"—cultural, economic and political development.

"*Think Black*"—loyalty and dedication to advancing the cause of Black America.

"*Black Is Best*"—absolute confidence in our ability to function as complete humans in any given situation and under all circumstances.

"*Black Is Beautiful*"—shameless appreciation for all that the black man was, is, and hopes to be.

"*Self-determination*"—at all times, the captains of our fate.

"*Separatism*"—integration will only fragment the community and destroy its power potential. Stay together and become strong together. Only then can the yoke of 400 years of servitude be cast off.

The analysis can be as endless as the slogans.

Mr. Earley spells out in practical detail what he sees as the programmatic aspects of the message of our black youth, including bloc voting, refusing to be bound by party labels in elections, indoctrination of the black family "in the principles and ideologies of active self-determination," black cultural and historical awareness, black economic development, black control of urban rebuilding, and redirection along constructive lines of the activity of black gangs. More important, he insists that older trained leadership must pool its skills and resources as never before to respond to the call of black youth for aid.

There is also sober advice for our more mature black brothers and sisters:

These suggestions are necessarily broad. They would certainly require close examination, and may in the end prove valueless. But, whatever goals may be developed, the black youth must be totally and uncompromisingly involved. It is their energy, their inventiveness, their dedication which must be harnessed. They are begging for responsible leadership. They want direction—goals. They recognize the social dynamic that exists today, and they know the role they must play. It is incumbent upon the black professional, the black intelligentsia, the black parent, the black worker to insure the black youth full enjoyment of their role in this social dynamic. They need us—we need them. Together.

"A little child shall lead them," a sacred book records. This prophecy may well be fulfilled in our time. How can we be other than grateful to the tens of thousands of young Jean Smiths and to "our Jean" in particular? Although I do not recall having ever met her personally, I feel that she is one of my own. Don't you?

Knowing the rich beauty of what we are is a continuous process and not a static fact. As with all voyages of discovery, there will be dead ends and retreats. But they are part of growth. We as black people must be willing to accept our rediscovered way of life, if we are to do our unique and far more substantial part in helping to lead our nation and our world.

CHAPTER SEVEN

The Need
to Organize

THE BLACK BROTHERS AND SISTERS WHO ATTENDED THE 1967
National Conference on Black Power in Newark, New
Jersey, took part in what was perhaps the most substantial
study symposium on the theme of power for the powerless
in the nation's history.

Throughout the three and a half days of study, more
than 100 papers were presented by scholars and professionals in small group workshops and then discussed; one
fact emerged as indisputable. The disorganization of black
communities, in terms of both customary attitude patterns
and interrelationships, *must* be overcome.

Several essays in *The Black Power Revolt* and Vincent
Harding's distinguished paper "The Gift of Blackness,"
which we shall examine closely in the next chapter, were
prepared for the 1967 National Conference on Black
Power. The key problem in the proposed publication of
the conference papers has been a general feeling among
those who prepared papers for study by the delegates

that they had advanced so far in their own thinking as a result of the conference that their papers no longer represented their points of view.

Power for the Powerless?

In each of the fifteen workshops at the 1967 National Conference on Black Power approximately eighty people worked together for the entire period of the conference. Their task was to reflect on the continuing powerlessness that marks practically every phase of our lives as black people.

The conference was limited to full-time participants, as coming and going could not create an ideal atmosphere for thoughtful self-examination. Observers of any kind were not welcomed, for spontaneous and unfettered give and take are impossible when all present are not taking the risks that such free interchange requires. The conference was open to all who could serve the most critical needs of our nation by sharing in a painful introspective examination of the persistent powerlessness in the common life of black Americans.

Each of those who prepared papers for the conference was asked to examine a specific aspect of our shared life, first, to discover why all our efforts had not created sufficient power for growth into self-sufficiency and self-respect. From this analysis of the subject areas listed as "Workshop Topics for the 1967 National Conference on Black Power," the writers then sought clues to how we might begin to develop in each of these areas some substantial measure of authentic power.

Workshop Topics for the 1967 National Conference on Black Power

Workshops	Coordinators
1. The City and Black People: Civic and Social Concerns	Lee Montgomery and Oswald Sykes
2. Black Power Through Black Politics: Local, State, and National	C. Sumner ("Chuck") Stone and Dan Watts
3. Black Power in World Perspective: Nationalism and Internationalism	Maulana Ron Karenga
4. Black Power Through Economic Development	Robert Browne
5. The Black Home	Nathan Hare
6. Black Power and American Religion	Reverend C. Lincoln McGhee
7. New Roles for Black Youth	Cleveland Sellers
8. Black Artists, Craftsmen, and Communications Personnel	Ossie Davis, Carol Green, and Florence Kennedy
9. Black Professionals and Black Power	Hoyt Fuller and Gerald McWhorter
10. Developmental Implications of Black Power	Dr. James Comer
11. Black Power and Social Change	John Davis and Lou Gothard
12. Fraternal Civic and Social Groups	Fay Bellamy and Grace Malone
13. Cooperation and Alliances	James Farmer and Vivian Braxton
14. New Trends for Youth	William Strickland
15. The Black Woman	Jorja English and "Queen Mother"

[*General Coordinator: Phaon Sundiata Goldman*]

The decision to use a study symposium as the format for the conference did not come easily. To reflect upon the roots of one's disease, malaise, or pathology is always a painful enterprise. Isaiah Robinson, President of the Harlem Parents' Committee, who served as Arrangements Chairman for the conference, half-jokingly asked during one of our lively planning-committee debates if any of those present knew the basic difference between a so-called "militant" and an Uncle Tom. He explained that all too often the crucial difference was that the so-called "militant," in an aggressive and sometimes apparently threatening way, simply *demanded relief!* Those present quickly grasped his point. We as black people have been breast-fed so long that we have not seriously come to grips with what it even means to have real power to determine for oneself one's own needs and then to have the reasonable capacity to fulfill those needs once one has determined them.

It is in this light that we must look, with a kind of limited appreciation, at the recommendations of the timely 1968 report of the President's Commission on Civil Disorders. If by some miracle all the prescriptions of the report were *given* to us as black people tomorrow, then the day after tomorrow there would be "bigger and more spectacular" civil disorders. The simple provision of more jobs, more housing, better education, better protection of persons and property, and far greater access to opportunities and relationships now available to white Americans would serve largely to build in greater dependence for black people and would thus serve to spawn even greater black self-hatred. As Dr. Charles Hamilton puts it, "If black people are simply *given* more handouts, this will only perpetuate the present status of ghetto colonialism."

What all men need in the most fundamental way is the power of self-determination. This power is precisely what black people have not had. In all the workshops of the 1967 National Conference on Black Power there was explicit awareness that, beyond any specific programs, black people need most the power to work, with substantial hope of success, for the fulfillment of their own, largely self-determined, destiny.

At the conference the story was told of a woman who had come before a judge to seek a divorce. Had her husband not provided for her? No. He had given her every material thing that she wanted, often in double measure. She had two cars and two fur coats. Whenever she expressed a need, she was treated as a Christmas tree. Another ornament was added. She was decorated in abundance. But she had not been provided for as a person.

"We do not want better housing. We do not want better schools. We do not want any more of anything. We simply want to be treated like *people*." This message is being made increasingly clear, as the smoke fades above the smoldering rubble of our cities. "Persons" have a sense of themselves. They experience a creative give and take with others. They recognize a sense of power over their own destiny. They know that they are more than "things." What all life needs is this power to achieve its own fulfillment.

Frustration is to have a goal but not the power or capacity to achieve it. Black men, women, and children in the United States have found frustration to be their daily lot. Black people want daily for a fair return for energies fully spent, but there are certain rewards for white men and other rewards for "others." Sometimes the reward is more, not less. Sometimes the black men receive the breaks. They are accorded a kind of preferential treatment. Whether they are given too much or too little, however, the general rule prevails: There are other rewards for "others."

The so-called "antipoverty" programs, for example, often favor the black poor over the poor who happen to be white. Or the exceptional black man may often get a more than even break. Yet, characteristically, a crucial ingredient is missing. He does not hold the reins. Others do *for* him; others decide. He is, after all, part of a world controlled by white men, the predominating goals of which are determined by white men. Black people have not had the power to control, to shape, or to insist even in those areas that pertain to their own immediate welfare.

Those with power decide. Those without power become what others decide that they shall or shall not be. A fundamental purpose of organization in the black community is to build decision-making power.

Organization for Liberation

In political and economic terms, to fulfill Martin Luther King's words—"Free at last, free at last! Thank God almighty, we are free at last!"—demands at the very least that black people should own and control their immediate environment. This goal was the primary concern of workshops 1 and 2 at the 1967 National Conference on Black Power. The first session of Workshop 1 was devoted to a discussion of "Who Should Control the Cities? Housing Ownership and Civic Investment." The first session of Workshop 2 was focused on "Who Should Control the Cities? The Politics of Control versus the Politics of Participation."

Freedom means reasonable capacity for self-determination. When others decide our needs, we experience frustration, and frustration, however modified or sweetened by the kindly care of others, will be forever the common daily lot of all black people as long as others *decide and plan* for us. We must organize in order to decide and plan for ourselves. As long as we are divided, others will determine and prescribe for our needs. The fifth session of Workshop 2, on black politics, dealt with the issue of "Coalitions *from* Power." We can only coalesce or unite equally with others *after* we have addressed ourselves to the task of developing our own group power.

Whenever in my continual travels I meet a black brother or sister, I smile and address him or her as "good Brother" or "good Sister." I find that this friendly and reserved greeting turns our brothers and sisters on. They seem to feel affirmed. After the venting of angry frustration at the tragic assassination of the greatest of our brothers (who was also this nation's greatest private citizen), I happened to greet in my customary way a sky cap in the airport of a major city. He stopped me and said what now amounts to a litany among us: "I wonder when our black brothers will learn that it isn't whitey; it's us. We need one thing. We need to get ourselves together."

As long as black people are divided, others will continue to control our lives. Once we get ourselves together, we'll be the most formidable force for good in our nation's life.

Getting ourselves together requires, quite frankly, a radical reassessment of who and what we are. It is painful to wean ourselves from the old and tested securities, however degrading they may be. Change is always a painful and highly uncertain thing. It is natural to cling to dependence, to the coattails of others, but it is far more mature and manly to will one's own growth, to fulfill the promise of our creation. We must do so, however, to achieve the capacity for our own self-development into independence and dignity, for our own good and for the good of all.

Liberation and self-determination involve the recognition of our own self-evident separateness. We must stop playing games with ourselves about the realities with which we have been living. Other ethnic groups take their separateness for granted and use it as the basis for all forms of equitable coalescence.

Harold Cruse, author of *The Crisis of the Negro Intellectual*, writes incisively on this point:

> . . . Every other ethnic group in America . . . has accepted the fact of its own social advantage. But the Negro's conditioning has steered him into that perpetual state of suspended tension wherein ninety-five per cent of his time and energy is expended on fighting prejudice in whites. As a result, he has neither the time nor the inclination to realize that all of the effort spent fighting prejudice will not obviate those fundamental things an ethnic group must do for itself . . . The American Negro has never yet been able to break entirely free of the ministrations of his white masters to the extent that he is willing to exile himself, in search of wisdom, into the wastelands of the American desert. That is what must be done, if he is to deal with the Anglo-Saxon as the independent political power that he, the Negro, potentially is.

Political and economic power must be rooted in a sense of unashamed, and indeed proud, black purpose. It was the Jewish philosopher Hillel who once said:

> If I am not for myself, who will be for me?
> If I am only for myself, what am I?
> If not now, when?

Clarence Lee Townes, the highest-ranking black man on the Republican National Committee staff, reminded those attending the tenth annual convention of the Southern Christian Leadership Conference of the paramount need for organizing *as black people* for effective political power: "Black folks will win acceptance from the larger society only by developing their own bases of power, not by submerging their unorganized and leaderless followers into coalitions dominated by other more solitary groups."

Paul Hathaway, staff writer for the Washington, D.C., *Star,* reported on August 16, 1967, Mr. Townes' remarks under the heading "Build Black Power Bases, Negro GOP Aide Asks":

> He said that since the Negro is unable to gain political power under the present political system, he must develop strength with his own ranks.
>
> Black power advocates favor the formation of black institutions and creation of black economic and political power as a means of creating far-reaching social changes. They have been critical of racial integration.
>
> ### Favors Ghetto Institutions
>
> "The ghetto is deprived of resources that could encourage the development of its own institutions or bolster them," Townes said. "Existing social agencies could serve the ghetto better if they lent political, technical and financial aid to the development of new social welfare institutions that would be under black management and black control."
>
> He said that once black social and political institutions have been formed, the ghettoes can then "bargain for a share of power over crucial institutional processes."
>
> "Programs such as the present anti-poverty program have done nothing to strengthen the ghetto's capacity to deal with its own problems," Townes declared, noting that it has contributed to the weakening of black community life by increasing fragmentation and dependency.
>
> Touching on the Democratic party's hold on the Negro vote, Townes said there is increasing evidence that the Negro is determined not to be "the captive of one-party politics."

Before a "blue-ribbon" group meeting under the auspices of the People's Settlement Association in Wilmington, Delaware, on April 4, 1968, Delaware's lone black state senator, Herman Holloway, Sr., spoke of the need for black political sophistication. He said that only a little sophistication should suggest several things: among them that black people should at least appear to be together and that they should assume a decisive role as the major independent political force in most local, state, and national elections. Such political power, Senator Holloway explained, could begin to afford black people the same capacity to direct their own lives that other groups have developed. "We cannot have power," he declared, "if we are not willing to admit the obvious; that we are a group, having legitimate interests as an independent group."

In a similar vein, we cannot have economic power unless we have far, far greater group purpose than we now have. William Cash, of New Jersey's black "Halo Wig" salon chain, preaches the gospel of black economic self-interest. He believes that only as blacks stand up with and for one another can black people become the independent force that makes for economic power. This motivation is precisely that of such men as C. C. Spaulding of the North Carolina Mutual Insurance Company and A. J. Gaston, Atlanta's black millionaire banker and operator of the famed Gaston motel enterprise.

Black businessmen—and white friends who would encourage them to grow in economic independence—might well appreciate and use to good advantage these words from the Philadelphia Student Non-Violent Coordinating Committee:

> Most black adults can talk about Black Power and Black self-determination, but we still depend for our bread and health on the white establishment. We can-

not get to our goal if this situation goes on. We must organize so as to change our black situation right away. We must organize so that we do not *need* or *have to* depend upon whites at all; so that we no longer are forced to accommodate and fulfill their goal. And this action of self-determination involves neither love nor hate for white people—but *our black survival.*

White people who would help us should be asked by us *not for program moneys but for organizing moneys* in order that we may "get ourselves together." Only with black collective purpose first may we begin to develop either economic or political power.

Building further on the admonition from Harold Cruse to accept our uniqueness as a basis for power, we as black people must overcome or correct the enfeebling notion that there are deeply *significant* differences of status or class among us.

"Class" Differences?

We black Americans have been taught to think that there is a class problem among us. There is. It consists in our belonging to what one of the delegates to the conference called "the black class" and our failure to take a realistic view of both its difficulties and opportunities.

Those who attended the National Black Power Conference in Newark were overwhelmingly middle-class in orientation, which came as a shock to some of those present. One young delegate, who was obviously threatened by the presence of so many people of professional training exclaimed, "They have taken over *our* cause!" The remark is suggestive of how the whites' divide-and-conquer mentality still dominates us and has been a major cause of our continued debilitation. Also present at the conference were black staff representatives from the Lemberg Center for the Study of Violence at Brandeis University. They knew from their studies—as did many others from their own wider experience—that the largest proportion of black militance is among professionally or academically trained black people. They are, after all, the ones who have been most disillusioned by meeting all the criteria that our white-controlled society has set up for success only to be found still "wanting" and "not ready."

Not long after the national conference a local meeting was held by key people who had attended the conference from the State of New Jersey. It was scheduled for 8:00 in the morning. Between twenty-five and fifty people were expected. By 7:30, more than twenty-five were present, about half of them wearing the new self-expressive garb. At 7:45 the meeting had to be moved to larger quarters. By 8:20 an estimated 250 people were present. The later arrivals, that is, those who came after 7:45 drove up in Cadillacs, Continentals and Austin-Healys. Some twenty-five physicians, more than a dozen lawyers, and a judge's wife were present in the assembly. When workshop discussions were reluctantly brought to a close just before 10:00, there was too little time remaining to give adequate attention to the discussion reports.

The notion that there are insurmountable class differences among us simply is not true. In a sense, there are, for example, no black middle-class people. Some black people are middle-class *oriented*. They tend to emulate values and behavior of the white middle class. The class structure in the United States is basically related to white, Anglo-Saxon, Protestant background. Roman Catholics and Jews are not wholly in, although some believe that they are. Even in England, where white Anglo-Saxon class structure received its roots, Benjamin Disraeli knew all too well that, although he was baptized, he was still considered an outsider: He was the Jewish Prime Minister of England.

The United States class system may be said to have at least four parts. There is the basic white, Anglo-Saxon, Protestant class system. Then there are somewhat parallel class structures for Jews and Roman Catholics. There is some give and take among these systems of stratification, but they cannot be accurately perceived as one system. There are gradations of difference—and indeed different values—between the levels of each of these ethnically related systems.

Having some interplay with each of these class systems is the system of stratification among black people. A disproportionate amount of discussion has been given in the literature to the supposedly superficial basis for class differences among black people. It has been an exercise in futility, for class differences may all be discovered, under dissection and scrutiny, to be superficial. One central fact emerges, however, about the black class system. It is generally perceived as lower than all the other systems. For the lowest-class white Anglo-Saxon Protestant perceives himself and is perceived as of higher status or

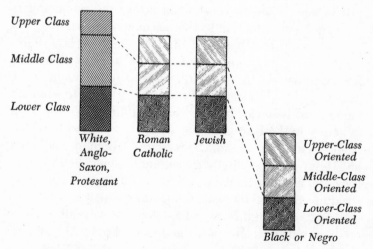

Figure 1. Valuation or Relative Place of Class Subsystems

worthier of more privilege than is a black man of the so-called "highest class." Figure 1 presents this situation diagramatically.

Black people as a whole have one basic problem, that of low status and relative lack of power related to a common experience of oppression, which must be dealt with by black people as a whole. When we are all in the basement of the American class system, it is a bit ludicrous to talk about whether one is on the top, middle, or bottom basement step. In dealing with it, we must not approach white Americans as beggars. Once we have made up our minds to stop kidding ourselves about so-called "class differences" and have begun to think of ourselves proudly simply as "black people," we shall have begun to alter the prevailing status and power relations to our advantage and for the better morality and greater maturity of the nation as well.

Black brothers and sisters, let's stop fooling ourselves and begin to move ahead wisely for our own liberation by working together as brothers and sisters determined to have freedom must do. We must cast off the destructive thinking patterns based on oppression that we have permitted to continue, and we must talk the talk and walk the walk of freedom together.

The Theory of Black Omniscience

"I happen to be a 'good Negro,'" says New York City Attorney Florence Kennedy. "This means that I accept the fact that I am *de jure** deprived. And if I had the choice between being *de jure* deprived or *de facto* deprived, I would choose to be *de jure* deprived."

In looking for solutions to the pressing problems of "urban" dislocation, some of those who are *de facto* deprived

---

* *De jure* means "by law," or in the considered judgment of those in power; *de facto* means "in fact" or having the actual effect of being.

—at least of the basic necessities of black people—have developed an interesting theory. It might be called appropriately the "theory of black omniscience." It is doubtless one result of the unconscious divide-and-conquer technique, with another, even more sinister, feature built into it. It holds that any black person, regardless of how he has been trained, if he has been trained at all, is competent to deal with any and all problems relating to black people. According to this bogus theory, although my training is in the social sciences, a medical team studying the black-related disease called "vitiligo" might rely upon me for medical advice!

This theory is precisely the type of thing that characterizes our so-called "antipoverty" and urban "renewal" efforts. The gimmick entitled "maximum feasible participation" of those served is an effective, if not deliberate, means to keep out black professionals and most black people with the skills to meet black people's needs. Most of the highly trained black people, who were born and grew up in the areas to be served, simply are not any longer residents of the areas of greatest poverty where their parents, relatives, and childhood friends live.

When government programs prescribe that the local municipal and social agencies providing the 10 per cent matching funds and services are to manage enterprises together with the residents of the affected area, a new kind of Jim Crow, or rape of black people, is achieved. The "fiddler payers" are the white-controlled municipal and social agencies. The black men and women of the greatest training, those who are best equipped to provide needed technical skills, besides being native to the environments and communities for which urban programs are designed, are largely eliminated from the planning and direction of these endeavors. That this omission is not simply an oversight is underscored by the rationale that has been built up for the belief that in the untutored and the untrained there is a great hidden and unused reservoir of talent. This untrained talent, so the rationale goes, must be given the massive resources both for the rebuilding of our cities and for the elimination of poverty from the land.

This theory is remarkable indeed! It supposes *rightly* that there is untutored and untrained talent that should be used. Why then is such talent not sought by industry? Why is it allowed to "drop out" of the schools? Why are not new agencies, like authentically community-oriented colleges, not created to develop these talents? This theory, which presupposes in effect that anyone who is black is omniscient or "omnicompetent," has the pernicious effect of making black people themselves think that there is little or no need to discipline their talents or to develop or acquire academic tools for the performance of specialized tasks. Furthermore, a misguided system of values is thus encouraged.

Several years ago, for example, a young man came to my office seeking help in securing new employment. He held a bachelor's degree and was in his mid-twenties. He had left an antipoverty job, at which he had been earning between $12,000 and $15,000 a year. He was in desperate need of employment. I told him that there was a possibility of an immediate job paying more than $7,000 a year. He refused to be interviewed for the job, saying that it would be beneath his dignity—despite pressing overdue mortgage and other payments—to accept any job, however temporary, below his former salary scale.

This experience was unsettling for me because it drove home a point, which I expressed to the young man. I explained that few people in the United States with only bachelor's degrees and still in their twenties make as much as $10,000. Major exceptions are the sons of bankers —and those on the so-called "antipoverty" payrolls. This situation is absurd.

The theory of black omniscience not only has been used to undermine the value system of both trained and un-

trained black people; it has also tended to limit the value of
Federal and foundation planning for our needs. Not long
ago, I participated in a small group meeting that included
several black people whose places of employment seemed
high, if not deep, in significant white structures of power.
These black men were well paid and well trained. But
initially they were clearly threatened by the presence of
several other black men who possibly had insights to share
with them.

At the end of the meeting, one of the government-
agency black men remarked to me that he wished he had
met the other black men earlier. "They really helped me.
We need to use each other" was his final assessment.

The tragedy was that these government employees were
made to feel by their agencies that they were *the* experts
on any and all matters pertaining to black people. They
were black "advisers" for decisions on how to spend millions of dollars to meet black folks' supposed needs and for
which white consultative help was almost entirely employed. At the relatively small old college that I attended
on the Charles River in Cambridge, Massachusetts, I was
taught that an educated man was one who knew that he
did not have all the answers but who also knew where to
find them.

Brothers and sisters, if we do not learn how to use one
another rightly and fully, what can we expect from others?
Furthermore, the mentality that claims the capacity to
shape unaided so much of the destiny of our brothers and
sisters clearly reflects a messianic complex. The last thing
that we need is a black messiah. We need to learn that for
our survival there is no such thing as "solo soul." We must
learn to be together.

In terms of consulting with one another, we *must* learn
that all of us have something to say. Even white folks
must learn this lesson; they may even follow our example,
once we have proved its validity. *Reflective, humble, un-*

*trained experience must always be used to complement
trained technical competence.* One is not a substitute for
the other, however. We must pool, whenever possible, our
diverse talents, competences, and experiences. We must
come further to learn that in every metropolitan area of
the nation broad leadership coalitions, composed of key
people from *every segment* of the black community, are
an absolute necessity for building an ethnic power base,
without which every other effort is almost certain to fail
or to achieve only very limited success.

The Dixwell House Dilemma

Another effective obstacle, not consciously designed but
nonetheless tragically dividing us, is the assumption that
there are at present no power components in the life of
the black community.

"We'll start from scratch," say many of the white-spon-
sored so-called "community organizers" and the white-controlled urban "redevelopers." Then often they set out to
do things that bring our conditions down to "scratch."
That there are potential power bases in the black community is apparent in our black churches; black welfare
mothers; teachers' unions; Elks and Masonic lodges; credit
unions; Greek-letter organizations; barbers' and beauti-
cians' and merchants' or business associations; and lawyers', doctors', and social and civic-interest groups.

Any proposed "organization" should begin with the
existing organizational elements, and only after they are
pulled together into working relationships should fresh
organization be undertaken. It is a gratuitous insult to
suppose that black people lack "organization." What we
most desperately need is to pull our many separate organizational components together. Few black people will
be found in any metropolitan area who are absolutely un-

related to any organized group, for, with our "extended family" ethos or group tradition, each of us is in one way or another related to something or other. New forms of organization, not rooted in white social-scientific preconceptions about black people, should be developed. Perhaps the basic "novelty" is the elementary assumption that the groups and the leadership potential *that already exist* represent the basic resources; they must be brought together.

This need for combination was a problem for the staff and community leadership of New Haven's only black social-service agency, the Dixwell Community Center, in 1967. There had been a number of local efforts at organizing. Indeed, the Dixwell Community Center staff was involved in a black leadership union, in professional associations, and in the actual organizing of so-called "grass-roots neighborhood groups." In spite of increased organization, however, the plight of black people did not improve; each new organization seemed no more able than the older ones to get things off the ground. The Heritage Hall Committee of the Dixwell Community Center, a thoughtful group of black men with widely diversified backgrounds, began a series of "brainstorming" meetings, or "think sessions," to assess the situation. Several significant conclusions emerged from their deliberations; they should perhaps be communicated to and reflected upon by black leadership in other cities.

1. *What constitutes an effective power base?* The group initially considered this problem the most critical. Can effective power be exercised for the black community's needs on a neighborhood basis? They reviewed the results of neighborhood organization as they had experienced it, and they read what literature was available. Their conviction was that such organization was nobly conceived in its purpose to give a sense of power to those most tightly gripped by a sense of powerlessness. Neighborhood orga-

nization could be used to secure better services and to pull local residents together for larger common purposes like improvement of local housing. *Local organization, however, had to be related to a larger black structure.* Although local organization should doubtless be continued and encouraged, it was concluded that some additional elements were required to form an effective power base to meet the basic needs of the black community. Equally important, the group found that local organizations generally failed to recognize that the problems of black people are fundamentally related not to neighborhood but to race. The group concluded that only through some mechanism for combining the power of the black community *as a whole* into a working force could the black residents of New Haven County begin to exercise truly effective power. The metropolitan area of New Haven County was thus recognized as the geographical unit for the exercise of black group power.

2. *How can we get black groups to merge their forces?* The traditional type of organization among black groups called for a formally designated leader. It was feared that the leaders of many groups in New Haven would not subordinate their own personal roles to the larger purpose. There was also the danger that white business or political leadership might "buy off" any single leader who could speak for the whole black community. Those who had attended the 1967 National Conference on Black Power in Newark were impressed by Maulana Ron Karenga's emphasis upon the need to develop what he called "operational harmony." "Operational harmony" does not require creation of a new organization. All groups keep their own leaders, their own programs, and their own identities. A coalition of the leaders is, however, created to conduct a dialogue and to make decisions for work in parallel and mutually supporting ways toward agreed-upon goals for the black community. This concept of operational har-

mony seemed to hold promise of aiding Greater New Haveners to overcome much of their traditional leadership problem. It was especially concluded that the mutually supportive potential of such a working relationship could do much for groups in the black community that could no longer afford to continue working in wholly or largely separate ways: such groups as the Muslims and the Christians, the Greek-letter college organizations, and the welfare-rights groups. Through the concept of "operational harmony" all would learn that they needed one another. There would also be a wholesome interchange of ideas, enthusiasm, financial and much-needed numerical support, technical competence, and perceptions that might help to weld the different segments of the black community into an interrelated, mutually rewarding, and mutually responsible family.

3. *What groups should be included in the coalition for operational harmony?* The answer quickly arrived at was "all groups." Any "leader" who had a roster of officers and a membership list was automatically considered a "key person" in the New Haven County black community.

If the most pressing requirement for developing effective group power for black people was at least a semblance of unity, then in some way all components of the black community had to be made to feel that they belonged to the black coalition. Purity of doctrine or of practice was not to be a criterion for participation in the coalition, any more than agreement on issues is a criterion of family membership. Common low status and lack of power were recognized as the central issues before black people everywhere. It is to address this issue that black people must get together. To build group power, no one can be omitted as an "Uncle Tom," a radical, "middle-class" oriented, or an outcast. To deal with the common condition imposed upon black people in America simply because they are black, all black groups must combine for group power.

The Heritage Hall Committee membership decided that, as in all families, black people should and must disagree among themselves but that to disagree does not mean to disavow. As world opinion and power sanctions are sought in the United Nations for dealing with world problems, so diverse black-community opinion and group sanctions were to be sought for dealing with common problems relating to development of black group status and power.

Just how could such a mechanism be introduced? People would not see any existing organization, however overarching, as one in which they had "ground floor" status. Nor would it be an easy matter to pull together the many segments of black leadership in New Haven County.

The problem of how to get things going was the final matter to which the Heritage Hall Committee at Dixwell House addressed itself.

4. *How can a metropolitan-area leadership coalition get started?* The question is one that every black metropolitan-area community in the nation must face and answer. For it seems certain that new, larger, and potentially all-inclusive and more effective coalitions for power are critically needed for our own survival and progress and for the nation's peace.

One member of the committee was the secretary of the Board of Education in New Haven. He reminded the group that, whenever the Board of Education wants to undertake major change or innovation, outside consultative help is sought. A clergyman in the group remarked that, when churches engage in major fund raising, they hire fund-raising consultants. An antipoverty aide added that "outside experts" were retained by the local antipoverty agency on many matters involving significant change. An employee of a major business firm was reminded of how his firm continually used management consultants to facilitate adjustments in its operations. Why not seek help, then, from the outside? There was an objection. Several people thought that there was more than sufficient local talent to do what had to be done. The simple answer eventually arrived at was that "a prophet is not without honor except in his own country." No one on the local scene, however brilliant or competent, could serve to get things off the ground, for he would not be listened to or heeded. An outside adviser was therefore necessary. Such help could serve the needs of black people, even as it serves thoughtful and responsible white people in critical situations.

I was called to the task of consultant to the Black Coalition of New Haven County in October 1967. The group has now gotten under way and has begun to come to grips with a number of short- and long-range problems. An initial question was how to organize for leadership. The group with which I met agreed that a consultant or expediter could work responsibly with only a very small steering committee. The decision was then made to elect a small but representative steering committee as the primary leadership instrument of the coalition.

The consultant's work with the steering committee is to assist its members in their continuing task of working with other leaders and not to act in any way as another leader in the traditional sense. It was agreed that the consultant should make no more than two public appearances a year before mass or family meetings of the black community. In this way, local leadership could be projected, and our tradition of following charismatic figures could be changed.

The consultant meets with the steering committee of the Black Coalition one or two evenings each month. Problems are reviewed, and strategy is planned. When it seems advisable, the consultant assists members of the steering committee in their meetings with individuals and groups. The steering committee is kept in the forefront. In order that some temporary excitement or enthusiasm—or a planned takeover—might not undermine the coalition's work, it is arranged that no major decisions are to be made without independent review by the consultant. This requirement forces the coalition into continued critical assessment of its efforts and promises to afford a much-needed preventive to disruption. The principal role of the consultant is to serve as expediter and gadfly in all that the coalition itself seeks to do.

The fact that the consultant is also an educator and what some call an "urbanist" brings to the coalition professional resources that are especially useful in its work. Whenever we organize, we as black people must be very careful not to accept too readily plans and goals set for us by those who have exercised kindly but nonetheless oppressive power over us. Those who have power may work willingly to see that the powerless are happy in their state of powerlessness, but they will not often take the initiative in helping the powerless to develop power. Power must always be appropriated, and the powerless must always come to recognize the crucial difference between what the Black Coalition membership in New Haven, Connecticut, calls "white niceness," on one hand, and the "empowerment of black people," on the other.

Rethinking Our Needs

An example of the kind of critical yet creative rethinking that the Black Coalition of New Haven has undertaken is reflected in its recent relations with the local antipoverty agency, Community Progress, Incorporated, or C.P.I. The coalition was aware of my own probing and criticism of much of the work of the Office of Economic Opportunity and the Ford Foundation, both of which have funded C.P.I. When I was asked for opinions on what to do in relation to C.P.I., my initial reply was typically consultative: What did the group wish to do? The answer was on two levels. It wished to bring an end to what it saw as sugar-coated white colonialism and exploitation, doubtless not deliberate, that C.P.I. seemed clearly to represent. The group also wished to be as politic as possible in relations with both board members and staff personnel of C.P.I. These practical considerations shaped the ultimate approach.

In my own intentionally proscribed catalytic work, I assisted the coalition in thinking through its response to an assault on C.P.I. that showed evidence of being politically inspired. The January issue of the Black Coalition's newsletter *The Heritage Hall Crow* spoke thus of the attack on C.P.I.:

> We know there are ills in CPI and it is not our purpose to defend it. However, many underprivileged people have been helped by CPI . . . CPI needs and should have an evaluation yearly! But not by a political yardstick—but by responsible and concerned elements in the community.

This guarded defense of C.P.I. had its good effect. Both white and black workers in the antipoverty agency were somewhat disarmed by the coalition's "defense." Nor were those who were helped by C.P.I. alienated by the coalition. Meanwhile, I prepared for the coalition a preliminary draft of the "Checklist for Community Services."

Checklist for Community Services

1. Number and per cent of poverty people (white, black, and total), 1963–1967.

2. Number and per cent of black staff for antipoverty agency.
3. Total black salaries and white salaries. Rank by race.
4. Total of other costs (including planning, administration, and consultation) paid to white and/or black agencies.
5. Income patterns in New Haven County over-all, 1963–1967 (white, black, and total).
6. Number and per cent of black people trained, placed, kept in employment by C.P.I. other than within the antipoverty agency itself or its subsidiaries.
7. Employment patterns in New Haven County (white, black, and total), 1963–1967:
   a) by occupation category;
   b) by industry category, including schools, colleges and city administration;
   c) by public and social agency category.
8. Number and per cent on welfare and unemployed (black and white), 1963–1967.
9. Number and per cent of migration from outside Connecticut, 1963–1967.
10. Indices of population shrinkage and increase by race and income level (1963–1967).

Basic Questions Concerning Agency Goals

1. What are you doing?
2. In what direction are you headed?
3. Why?
4. How can you tell whether you are getting there?

A moment's glance at the checklist should be more than enough to bring into serious question many of the program-funding procedures of so-called "antipoverty" and "urban improvement" endeavors in all our cities. The primary question it raised for the coalition's work was just how much progress in what specific areas relating to poverty and to urban rebuilding must we make each year —and for what over-all time span—in order to create equality in employment and other aspects of urban life for the disadvantaged? It was the coalition's conviction that this elementary question had neither been clearly posed nor adequately answered by those who funded New Haven's antipoverty or urban-improvement agencies. Indeed, it was agreed that, if this one question had been dealt with honestly in any city, far different personnel, programs, and principles would now be in use.

Two steps were therefore taken. The coalition demanded "an immediate decision to orderly discontinue C.P.I. through a planned phase-out." Then the Black Coalition sought and began to receive two kinds of funds. It received seed funds for its own appraisal and priority planning for New Haven's hard-core human needs. It also received some funds for supporting neighborhood groups in providing indigenous services that, although they would not eliminate poverty, would provide for simple survival with less indignity.

In less than six months, the Black Coalition had begun to set a new pattern for black community action. It was beginning to look at the over-all needs of New Haven's black community for the first time, and it had begun to receive enabling funds for this purpose. Perhaps most important, on April 3, 1968, the President of Yale University announced that Yale would respond to the local urban crisis through the Black Coalition. This announcement is a significant breakthrough in that at last black people were being recognized by white institutions as capable of managing their own immediate destiny.

Despite the fact that New Haven had previously been

considered a model for urban planning, the needs of black people had not been met at all satisfactorily—ample evidence of serious planning deficiencies. The Black Coalition so far has pinpointed several of these limitations, noting five false assumptions that must be eliminated in our work together as black people.

First, there is the false assumption that cities are only physical complexes. New Haven has become a "symbol of vitality" in some of its building design. But black people are worse off in relation to the community as a whole today than they were when massive physical renewal began. Cities must be viewed first as complexes of people. Urban planning must be recognized as planning largely for black needs since growing majorities of those representing urban needs in the most acute way are black people.

Second, there is the false assumption that "traditional poverty" is the basic problem in the black community. Lack of control over their immediate destinies—including fair opportunities for employment and chances to create or demand school environments conducive to learning by black children—is a continuing condition of black New Haveners. Despite massive "antipoverty" and "urban education" projects, the job picture does not improve, and black children drop out increasingly from the schools. The black community's basic need is less for sophisticated planning than for perhaps "rough" but surely "ready" power.

Third, there is the false assumption that the exercise of leadership must be conventional. The Black Coalition rejects the traditional "hang up" devices that stand in the way of getting work done at so many black meetings: for example, *Roberts' Rules of Order* and the notion that leadership must come only from the top. Black-managed plantations are no ideal substitute for white ones. Whoever is willing to do the job at hand is recognized as the initiator and expediter. Leadership and power must be where the work resources are. Every one needs all the others. Discussion emphasizes the one thing that counts most: areas of actual or possible agreement. Active efforts are made to find new areas of common agreement, as differences come to seem too unimportant to block the paramount need for black cooperation for freedom.

Fourth, there is the false assumption that young black firebrands are simply a nuisance. There is essentially only one label for us all: "brothers." Some brothers may be in desperate need of our help. It is clear that we must relate to them. The group quickly came to see the need to embrace its much younger brothers and sisters in a wholly responsible way. It was believed that, if indeed any had gone astray, it was because older black brothers and sisters had failed to relate to them and to listen to them sufficiently. Criticism of what one dislikes should not forestall acceptance, understanding, and development of responsible relationships that provide a basis for influencing the lives of others and of being influenced by them.

What is said here about our youth applies in a broader way also to our older brothers and sisters. We cannot condemn those who may not have come as far as we have in terms of black self-awareness. Just how long has any of us been working hard at being "together" in the new spirit, which is not, at the time of this writing, more than two years old? We must be far more patient toward and accepting of one another.

Fifth, there is the false assumption that the black community can be dealt with productively in piecemeal fashion. All decisions affecting black people are essentially pervasive, in that what affects one part of our community affects the whole. The details of "model cities" or antipoverty programs should be discussed by the entire black community.

Mutual Reinforcement

The February issue of *The Heritage Hall Crow* underscores black group interrelatedness and interdependence:

> After a family leadership meeting, the Black Coalition called for a phase-out of CPI. The group said, "the mounting unrest in our cities points to peril for the nation—that CPI by its own admission has f⁻ ⸱ ⸱ to involve Black people in a meaningful way to t⸱⸱⸱ · dignity of self-development."
>
> The Black Coalition's position is that "a new concept of dealing adequately with poverty problems must embrace the idea of self-determination. Black organizations at the neighborhood level must be funded in order that they can work to resolve some of their problems."
>
> The Coalition listed six necessary steps that must be taken in the phase-out:
>
> 1. An immediate decision to orderly discontinue CPI through a planned phase-out.
>
> 2. A commitment to reorganize the entire concept of attacking poverty and deal with causes in a meaningful way rather than innovations that are not effective.
>
> 3. Provision of a planning grant to deal effectively with the Black and non-Black hard core and "grass root" ghetto dwellers.
>
> 4. Properly define the economic needs and skills of people who are presently locked in the inner city.
>
> 5. Provide for Black workers and sensitive skillful whites of CPI to be maintained in capacities fitting their talents and skills so as to utilize their past experiences where possible.

6. Develop a means for broad black community participation by involving the black institutions, black middle class and "grass root" people in programs to improve dignity, respect, and aspirations of black people.

The spokesman said, "This is a far more realistic approach to the problems of poor people and it is the kind of effort that will solve our nation's problems of rebellions and revolution."

The Black Coalition will conduct two meetings to discuss the new concept of "neighborhood determination."

1. A family leadership and interested citizens meeting Thursday, February 28th, 7:30 P.M. at St. Luke's Church—111 Whalley Avenue.

2. A meeting involving the white community on February 29th—same time and place.

Yale University's recognition of the coalition as the agency best suited to plan for black needs was only part of the immediate result of the Black Coalition's February 28 and 29 family and public meetings. Planning and exploratory work with public-school leaders has begun unofficially, and it is anticipated that the Black Coalition may set the tone for a major redirection of the educational enterprise in New Haven.

In every metropolitan area in the nation, broad-based, open-ended, black leadership coalitions must be formed; they can build on such experiences as those of Dixwell House in New Haven. During the first seven months of the New Haven County Black Coalition's existence, it has set a worthy example of operational harmony and mutual support for Black America both to emulate and to extend.

Furthermore, we must relate to one another through such mechanisms as the National Conference on Black Power. It was the 1967 National Conference on Black

Power at Newark, New Jersey, that did most to legitimize and encourage the new mood of togetherness and harmony necessary for black power and freedom. In my *Ready to Riot* (1968), some of the gross misconceptions about that historic conference have been dealt with. Chuck Stone, in his essay "The National Conference on Black Power," included in *The Black Power Revolt*, writes:

> History will ultimately enshrine this great event as one of the finest efforts of black people to emancipate themselves psychologically as well as politically and economically from the white man's enslavement. "Let's get our minds straight" and "we've got to be a 'together' race before we can achieve real power in this racist society" were two themes recurring constantly in discussions among the delegates. (p. 198)

The emphasis was upon what we as black people must do for ourselves. The more than 1,000 delegates to the conference almost wholly forgot about what white people might do to facilitate our struggle for freedom. They recognized that the responsibility for our liberation and the fulfillment of the nation's future rests primarily with black sisters and brothers working *together*.

Chuck Stone concluded:

> July 20, 1967, Newark, New Jersey, must be remembered as the day when one of the most representative sections of black people—the young, middle-aged, elderly, rich, poor, the Protestant, Catholic, Muslim, agnostic, militant, moderate, conservative, the laborer, businessman, college student, writer, social worker, teacher, secretary, janitor, doctor, lawyer, minister, government employee, politician, public official, policeman, fireman, journalist, actor, hustler, numbers banker, waiter, salesman, real estate broker

and the unemployed—all came together at the National Conference on Black Power to write the boldest and most radical chapter in the black man's four-century-old struggle to be a true equal among equals. . . .

America doesn't know it yet, but she is going to feel for a long, long time the effects of what those 1,000 independently minded black folks did in Newark, New Jersey, for four fateful days. (p. 198)

In the chapter that follows, we shall gain at least a glimpse of what good lies in store for our nation as a whole, thanks to current efforts by black folks to "get ourselves together."

CHAPTER EIGHT

Healing
the Sick

A PERSISTENT THEME THROUGHOUT THE FIVE DAYS OF national mourning for Martin Luther King was expressed by Coretta King, as she spoke in a restrained and unembittered way of the sickness of American society.

Black Americans must face the fact that American society is sick partly because we as black people "have left undone those things which we ought to have done, and have done those things which we ought not to have done." Three courses are always theoretically open to the oppressed. They may change the society that oppresses them. They may leave that society. Or they may remain oppressed. The so-called "Uncle Toms" (who would remain oppressed) and the black nationalists (who would leave America) are thus, in one sense, reasonable men. But the oppressed cannot simply buy into the oppressive system "as is" and hope at the same time to be truly free. Furthermore, to refuse to help recall our nation to its roots in these perilous times is to forfeit a share in the fullest fruits of freedom.

The United States today needs precisely the social, political, civic, and moral change and adaption that can come only from worthy and determined black Americans.

That white America today is *wholly* indifferent to the plight of black Americans or to the needs of men throughout the world is untrue. That there is altruism in white America is clear at every hand. It gives more foreign aid than all the other nations of the world combined, and at home it has a larger budget for relief than does any other nation. It must be recognized that it is not the heart of America that is diseased but rather its sight.

Lest we forget, some white people have been "nice" to us as black people ever since we have been a part of this nation. But even their perception of us—and of many other groups—has been as of children or dumb animals. Like the woman whose husband treated her like a Christmas tree, we have been both received and put aside in such a manner as one deals with things.

A New Reality

"God, it must be terrible not to be born black in this day and age," writes the Afro-American novelist Ronald Fair. He refers to the subtle but deeply blinding—even though charitable—arrogance with which much of white America is afflicted. It renders those who share in its pretensions, born of a tradition of unchecked power, insensitive to realities that are self-evident to others. To be born white in America, with its heritage as chief dog in a kennel all its own, means to be born with an inherited affliction of sight. For the world is manifestly not what it seems to be in white America's eyes. Ronald Fair's words also refer to the saving marginality and urgent responsibility of those who have been born black in our increasingly myopic land.

Vincent Harding, in his paper entitled "The Gift of Blackness," delivered to the workshop on black power and

American religion at the 1967 National Conference on Black Power, amplifies the theme implicit in the words of Ronald Fair:

> I think that [there is] the growing recognition by Afro-Americans of the possibility that within the heart of our blackness there is a gift, a gift in the most marvelous Biblical sense of the word. Not the pleasant, pointless, painless tinsel-wrapped experience that we think of when we think of gifts, nor the romanticized gifts claimed by so many oppressed people to relieve the deadliness of man's existence. Rather, when I speak of a gift being at the heart of blackness in this land, I speak of gift in terms of the tough, hammered-out, often brutal experience which nevertheless produces a new reality, a new reality that may benefit the entire society and the entire world—to say nothing of the benefit that it might bring to those who call themselves the Church.

What is this "new reality" of which Vincent Harding speaks? Although Vincent Harding does not explicitly use the term, it may be described as *the driving and unalloyed will for wholeness for human life.*

If we as black men wish to become free—and if white America wishes to be healed of its own sickness and to grow into maturity—then all who call themselves "responsible" men must challenge and command black men to do their unique and crucial part to make total American life far more nearly what it should be. Somehow, the gift of blackness—this driving and unalloyed will for wholeness of human life—must be recognized and used for the common good of all.

One might well ask: If there is truly a gift of blackness, why have we not enjoyed its benefits before? Why have black men not reminded us of this precious gift, so vital to our national self-realization? In part the answer is that the gift was always there but the appropriate hour had not come. The gift of healing, which black America must now exercise for itself as well as for others, depends on our acceptance of our black selves. As long as we sought to be other than ourselves, the gift could not freely be recognized. Indeed, rather than a gift, it was to some degree in times past—and still is today to black people who have not gained self-awareness—a burden.

For the sake of sheer survival black men in the past have often hidden from reality. Such was the devastating pain of our lot in this short-sighted land. Nevertheless, more than thirty years ag : black poet Langston Hughes—one voice among many others—spoke what Vincent Harding calls the "new reality," of the America that can yet be. Today, perhaps, we may hear with greater understanding the prophetic words of Langston Hughes. They are at once radical and conservative, calling upon America to conserve and to reaffirm *its roots,* which is what the term "radical" suggests. In "Let America Be America Again" he wrote:

Let America be America again.
Let it be the dream it used to be.
Let it be the pioneer on the plain
Seeking a home where he himself is free.

(America never was America to me.)

Let America be the dream the dreamers dreamed—
Let it be that great strong land of love
Where never kings connive nor tyrants scheme
That any man be crushed by one above.

(It never was America to me.)

O, Let my land be a land where Liberty
Is crowned with no false patriotic wreath,
But opportunity is real, and life is free,
Equality is the air we breathe.

(There's never been equality for me,
Nor freedom in this "homeland of the free.")

Say who are you that mumbles in the dark?
And who are you that draws your veil across the stars?

The mumbling voice replies:

I am the poor white, fooled and pushed apart,
I am the Negro bearing slavery's scars.
I am the red man driven from the land,
I am the immigrant clutching the hope I seek—
And finding only the same old stupid plan
Of dog eat dog, of mighty crush the weak.

Hughes continues his catalogue of those who are oppressed through three long verses. He claims many
"others" as his own, in the common humanity of all.

Black yearning for—and loyalty to—the best in this
nation's dream is also expressed in Hughes' poem:

O, let America be America again—
That land that never has been yet—
And yet must be— . . .

O, yes,
I say it plain,
America never was America to me,
And yet, I swear this oath—
America will be!

This poem, written in 1936, is an American—and world
—classic. It must be read in full if its depth is to be
comprehended.* Of this black gift that holds forth the
promise of wholeness for our nation and that of all mankind, of this "new reality," Vincent Harding writes: "We
need others—as is always the case with gifts—we need
others to help us to perfect this gift. But it is ours."

Vincent Harding provides a portrait of our predicament
as black people that at once indicts white America and
lays a burden upon black America:

> After we had moved out of the South, and after
> many of us had deserted the old churches, we could
> no longer sing about Heaven because we didn't really
> believe in it any more, and we could no longer sing
> about the hopes of the North because we had been
> there and all of our hopes there had been crushed.
> And we couldn't believe in the God of the Sunday
> school books because he was white, and that sure
> wasn't right. Still, there was faith. Out of that ex-
> perience of moving with the trains and moving with
> the migrations and moving to the North to the hope-
> lessness and the strangeness and the sadness, there
> was yet a tough faith that gave us a capacity to en-
> dure and to produce a literature—in the blues—which
> surely must be called a kind of protoexistentialism.
> For if there was ever any situation in which people
> could say, "Hell is your neighbor," black people in
> America have known this. If there was ever a
> group of people who could say, "life is an ab-
> surd existence with no exit," black people in
> America, especially once we got North, could say
> this. Then in the midst of this saying and in the fire

* It appears in *The Poetry of the Negro, 1746–1949: An Anthology*,
Langston Hughes and Arna Bontemps, eds. (Garden City, N.Y.: Double-
day, 1949). Copyright 1938 by Langston Hughes. Renewed. Reprinted
by permission.

of this experience, we began to sing again some kind
of strange faith that was trying to say what it meant
to live where there was no exit and the white neighbors were indeed the agents of Hell. Out of this came
the blues. The blues was our statement of faith,
strange faith, sometimes convoluted faith, sometimes
pointless faith, but still faith. And the blues said,
"feeling tomorrow just like I feel today," somehow
knowing that tomorrow was going to bring nothing
more than what was being experienced in a thousand
bitter todays. Somehow it seems to me that this kind
of experience—the experience of living in a situation
that can be described only as absurd, and yet having
the faith to continue reaching into that situation and
looking for some means by which to endure—that this
could not have happened without a gift that we might
call faith.

We as black people have for 400 years experienced the
American absurdity in which the color of one's skin rather
than one's humanity determines such basic matters as life
and death, good and evil. It is up to us who know the
barrenness of a hope not harnessed to a driving will to
make faith become for us and for all in America and in
our world truly "the substance of things hoped for, the
evidence of things unseen."

We as black people must turn away from the past cling-
ing to false security, which was rooted in the simple need
to survive. We must now move toward the salvation of
ourselves through dedication to the healing of the sick
society in which we live; for this healing we alone have
the power. We must move away from the escapism associated with our need to survive and with white America's
need to be "white" *as an end in itself*. We must awaken
our land to a new vision of a society that is first and last
humane.

The Rediscovery of Truth

Another manifestation of the gift of blackness—which must be used for the healing of America's sickness—is the ability to distinguish between true and false spirits.

During the days of mourning for Dr. King, marches were held in a number of cities. More than 25,000 white and black men marched in Newark, New Jersey, alone. They wore black arm bands and buttons bearing the words "I Care." But *what* do they care about?

White America has cared enough to keep black Americans alive for all the years of our presence in America. There are large numbers of city dwellers who pay more for food and for medical and cosmetic care for their pet animals than for themselves; they care. The American public pays astronomically for "freedom" in Southeast Asia and for the survival needs of black people in our cities. It cannot be said realistically that America's heart is marked by anything other than the tangibly expressed sentiment "We Care." But simply to care is not enough; caring must be based upon an adequate perception of reality.

Unfortunately, men who are bound by the arrogance and pretensions of unchecked and unequal power relations tend to see as real only what bolsters their power. Truth to those who may be called "all-powerful" tends to be distorted by convenience and self-interest.

In the fulfillment of its historically consistent role of legitimizer of the *status quo,* for example, institutional Christianity has given shape to a conception of truth that permits distortion of reality. Correction must come from those of us with the awesome responsibility of blackness.

For centuries the knowledge of God, essential to the Christian or religious life, has been seen as the comprehension or acceptance of what was considered to be objective truth. This is precisely where we are today.

Yet, to the ancient Hebrews, who gave our Christian theology its basic shape, religious knowledge was not a thing of the intellect. It was knowledge as relationship. To know God meant to *enter into* God's life and to become one with and in Him. It was such knowledge as when a husband "knows" his wife and a wife "knows" her husband. The verb "to know" is essential to teachings about Christ's birth. St. Joseph is said to have lived with our Lord's mother but "knew her not" (St. Matthew 1:25).

The Church today must discover afresh a lesson long forgotten: what it means to know God. Hebrew thought suggests that to know God goes beyond intellectual assent to participation in God's life and the life of each and every man who also lives in Him.

When mere intellectual assent is taken as the essential ingredient of the Christian life, violence is done to human life, and the illusion that we are safe is fostered. When we rediscover that knowledge of God is essentially life lived *in Him*, then the Church can regain its integrity.

The experience of truth, in both its secular and sacred aspects, involves a sense of relationship. We cannot comprehend any truth fully unless we are willing to risk enough of ourselves to relate to others. The experience of truth, viewed in this light, is part of a process of growth and discovery. Truth itself is always open and tentative. It requires giving of ourselves, and thus it is that people whose lives are closed and unembracing cannot deal adequately with truth.

Tom Wicker described, in *The New York Times* on March 26, 1968, what he sees as a "kind of mindless racism." The title of Wicker's article is "In the Nation: Meet Benjamin Banneker." Banneker, as noted earlier, was a, black scientist and abolitionist. Wicker tells of Banneker's

having published annually after 1792 a widely used al-
manac, a copy of which he sent to Thomas Jefferson together with a letter chiding Jefferson for his inconsistent
views on the institution of slavery. Wicker writes, "It is
too bad that so few today, white or black, know anything
about this remarkable early American." He continues:

> That is true also of, say, Dr. John S. Rock, a Boston
> physician who also became, before the Civil War, the
> first black man admitted to legal practice before the
> Supreme Court; nor do many Americans realize that
> a black man came over the Atlantic with Columbus,
> well before the Mayflower; another explored the West
> with Lewis and Clark, and another went to the North
> Pole with Peary.
>
> Tom Johnson of this newspaper has just returned
> from several months in Vietnam during which he
> made a close study of the attitudes of the black sol-
> diers who make up more than 60 per cent of the Army
> there. One of his most curious findings was that many
> of them believed that in Vietnam, Negroes were for
> the first time getting a chance to prove themselves as
> fighting men, and that this belief pushed many of
> them to excel as soldiers.
>
> Few of them knew, Johnson found, that thousands
> of Negroes served under George Washington in the
> American Revolution and under Andrew Jackson in
> the War of 1812; that black troops acquitted them-
> selves well on both sides in the Civil War, and that a
> large number of the storied cavalrymen who cleared
> the Indians from the old West were black men.
>
> This is just one more result of the all-white orienta-
> tion of American society and culture—that most deep-
> seated and unquenchable form of racism which is
> neither malignant nor expressed, but unconscious. It
> is this orientation which has virtually eliminated from

American education any study of the origins, the development, the cultural and social contributions and even the simplest history of more than 10 per cent of the population.

This all-white education (a matter quite distinct from the question of pupil segregation) has been responsible for what James Baldwin called "A feeling of no past, no present and no future" in Negro children. It has made black soldiers in Vietnam unaware that they are part of a long and valorous tradition, and it has obviously been a large factor in the lack of self-esteem noticeable in many older Negroes.

The Subtle Effects

It is equally obvious that the practical expunging of the Negro from the record of the past is bound to have had its subtle effect on white attitudes. If white men do not know that black men helped with American independence and pacify the continent, it is a lot easier to talk glibly of "giving" the Negro his rights only when he has "earned" them.

Representative James Scheuer of New York has been looking into all this with a view to establishing a commission on Negro history and culture. No doubt that would help; but the greater need is for school boards, teachers' associations and textbook publishers to take some direct, practical action against this kind of mindless racism.

Plato emphasized the need for continuing confrontation with truth throughout one's life. But the tragedy of so much of white America is that it has so very much falsehood to unlearn. The President's Commission on Civil Disorders is said to have run into significant difficulty with some of its consultative personnel on the issue of just how

much truth the American public can take. When we as a
people cannot be trusted with the truth, something clearly
has gone wrong. Yet there is evidence at almost every
hand of our unwillingness to deal freely with it.

Ernest Dunbar, black senior editor of *Look*, wrote in the
April 16, 1968, issue about the strange inability of American white people to comprehend elementary truth. His
article entitled "Memo to L.B.J.—See America First . . . If
You Can" tells how this inability makes a substantial difference between travel in Europe and in the United States
for black people:

> When I fall into a conversation with a Dane over
> *Schnapps* or with a Yugoslav awash with *slivovitz,*
> they don't ask me what Stokely Carmichael means by
> his latest statement. And that's a gas, Mr. President.
> It just so happens that when I've seen him on televi-
> sion, though, he has usually been speaking in English,
> and I've always found it hard to understand why
> casual white strangers in America ask me to interpret
> his remarks. Also, I've been in Europe numerous
> times, and no European has ever asked me "What do
> you people want?" Strangely enough, Mr. President,
> Europeans seem to sense what we want.

Martin Luther King spoke plain truths to America's
ears, and during his lifetime some people heard. Others
began to hear, at least for a moment, after his assassination. Still, his elementary message that war, poverty, and
racism are all caused by the great sin of seeing human life
as a means rather than an end seems too difficult for some
to comprehend. Which part of it is difficult? Is it that he
as a black man had the audacity to speak out on issues
like American foreign policy that do not directly touch
upon race relations? He spoke words of healing, words that
reflect a will for wholeness for human life, when he de-

clared, perhaps more vigorously than any other man in America, that our policy in Vietnam is morally and politically wrong. "I speak," he said, "not out of anger, but out of love for America and out of the hope that America can change." But the almost absolute power of this nation has corrupted the minds of its citizens, creating an inability to distinguish sophistry from truth.

Because we as black people have not had a vested interest in the complacent distortions peddled for too long in our schools and in our public excuses for slowness to change at home and for aggression and blindness abroad, we may perhaps, as Vincent Harding suggests, "be able to perform the tremendous task of facing America with the truth, the setting-free truth, the bitter medicinal truth." He explains:

Somehow it appears that here in America, if my own experience bears any truth, one of the tremendous gifts that black people have for this society is not in most of our textbooks on sociology, political science and history. The joys of democracy and the ever upward-and-onwardness of the American society have little meaning to the majority of those whose parents were slaves. This is what the late Langston Hughes meant when he said in his marvelous poem, "America, you've never been America to me." This is what Stokely Carmichael meant when at the Spring Mobilization for Peace he read American history from the black side, and charged the American people with genocide. He read it in terms of the burning of the Indians by the Puritans while they gave thanks to God. He read it in terms of the concentration camps that were created for these first families. He read American history in terms of the rape of Mexico. He read American history in the light (or darkness) of the crushing of the Cuban rebellion in 1898. He

read American history through the destruction of the
Philippine Revolution in the years that followed
Cuba. He read American history in terms of the constant North American domination of the Latin nations. He read American history out of the eyes of a
black man, eyes that have witnessed thousands of
community lynchings and millions of more gradual
brutalizations. As a result, Carmichael concluded
each paragraph by declaring, "We charge genocide."

If there is to be healing in this land we love—a love
sometimes attested by our bitter wrath—we black folks
must become this nation's teachers. If this nation is to
"hear it like it is"—and all men need to have their lives
grounded in truth—then somehow we black folks must
"tell it like it is."

Our young people must stay in school to learn the tools
that only the schools can impart. We must establish in
every city and town community building and learning
centers like those being developed in Philadelphia and
elsewhere. These centers enable the young to learn American and black history "straight" and facilitate in many
ways the development of black dignity, pride, solidarity,
and hope.

We must encourage our black scholars and insist that
the nation heed them, and we ourselves must relate to one
another far more extensively. If we are to speak the truth
to heal this nation, we must insist that those among
us who have words to speak do speak them. We must
comprehend the healing message of those whose lives
have been so greatly marked by pain that their words have
taken on an anguish that attests their deep humanity.

If we are to heal by compelling a confrontation with
truth for the nation, we must discipline ourselves against
pseudo truth. The mere desire for truth is no substitute for
its acquisition. We must engage in the difficult double task

of studying truth alloyed with falsehood and then of disengaging one from the other. This task is the painful price of our freedom. For only by changing the society that has oppressed us can we hope to be truly free. We need a black mystique and a black mythology, and we must build them with sophistication.

We must work not simply to change curricula but to change the nature of our schools as well, so that learning can be related to life. We must thus work to see that disciplined growth into new awareness by the masses of our people is regarded as academically relevant and rewarded with traditional academic honors.

The marginal nature of our existence in American life makes us as black men potentially among the nation's best doctors. People who are *in* a society although not *of* it may bring a saving objectivity to that society's life. We have also a kind of dramatic distance, being removed, in a sense, to the balcony of American life, where we can see and comprehend life at the center of the stage better than the participants can. A sick America should call forth the latent powers of the black physician in its midst. If the nation is to be healed, black men must bring the saving truths that promise healing and wholeness for the people of this land.

Burning Coals

Our gift of blackness includes its most painful aspect, gift of prophecy. The handling of this gift is like the handling of burning coals. Who wishes to look into the future and see the judgments inextricably intertwined with precarious growth into fulfillment? Not I. Yet biblical prophecy dealt not with the future but with the present. Vincent Harding writes:

> The prophet has been described as "one who sees beneath the surface and clearly apprehends the inner

hidden trend of events." The prophet in Israel, rather than focusing on the future, often spoke most cogently to the present. Everywhere, he is one who speaks honestly to the people concerning what they say they believe in, and who speaks of what will happen to them if they continue to deny their own vows. I think that many black men in America have been granted the painful position of prophets. For there is surely a need for prophecy in this land today, and we are those who have often been most free to speak with clarity and authority of the unfaithfulness *now* and the fire *next time.*

In a meeting with a group of executives from a major paper-processing concern, I heard many comments that government equal-opportunity programs are and will continue to be miserable failures because they cannot "force" the closing of the economic gap between white and black people. As I listened to the sentiments of these altruistic men, I detected clear resentment at being forced to hire men whom they judged unqualified to do the company's work. In fact, instance after instance was cited to show how "forced hiring," according to arbitrary codes, had worked to the detriment of both the company and the black men who had been hired.

As usual whenever I meet with decision-making committees, I was asked to give an initial overview of the employment situation and to suggest some of its meaning and possibilities. This task always involves a kind of prophecy. I pointed out, first, that the job plight for black people is not getting better; second, that bottom-of-the-ladder "plant work" (which is the only kind this firm had been asked by the government to open) is not the kind most urgently needed by black people; third, that all companies, either actively or by passive acceptance, have been engaged in the social process that has created our present explosive conditions; and, fourth, that simply meeting the government's demand for "equal opportunity" can at best only prevent things from getting worse and that this demand does not take into consideration the benefit to others of the handicap imposed upon black people in the past. Indeed, the Federal government itself, in spite of several obvious agency exceptions, is by no means an "equal opportunity" employer. I explained that this fact is understandable for many reasons, not the least of which is that equality as a goal has built-in self-defeating aspects. What is needed is *equity* for all. I have discussed this issue at some length in my *Ready to Riot* (1968).

After my presentation, those present were asked to recount their experiences and perceptions in hiring black people. As they spoke, I tried to be as "supportive" as possible with smiles and nods. When the rounds had been made, I asked if any person present could suggest any difference between what had been said by the company executives and the tenor of my opening remarks.

One sales executive asked to combine what he believed that I had said with his own personal conviction. Here is the essence of his summation:

I, for one, do not like to have my hand forced to do anything. Perhaps none of us do. But the hiring of black people in such a way as to overcome our previous socially acceptable and unconscious discrimination is in our self-interest. Perhaps the government agencies should have hammered away at this self-interest aspect of the issue. It is in our self-interest not to have black desperation be such as to endanger the safety of this building. It is in our self-interest that the nation is secure enough for us to stay in business. It is in our self-interest that the employment rate is high enough to make our business, and business generally, more profitable.

But, in addition, I hear you saying that "noble-purposed" people like those of us in this room are criminally engaged in robbing our local citizenry by having such inequitable employment practices as to endanger the public safety and create undue welfare, policing, and other extraordinary social maintenance costs for which the public must pay. This gives me an eerie feeling.

This all leads me to believe that unless some company like our own can take the initiative locally to come up with some kind of initial plan, study, or statement, which may spark some vastly new and far more realistic and workable approach to black employment opportunity, we are headed for dark days, indeed.

Here was a kind of prophecy, perhaps the best kind, in that it was voiced by one who should himself heed it.

It is absolutely essential for those of us who are to fulfill the awesome task of prophecy in this deceptively affluent and beleaguered land to know the difference between prophecy and simple "sounding off." If one's purpose is simply to express plainly and accurately one's feelings, that is one thing. If it is to change the attitudes and actions of others, however, then some sophistication and artistry are required. Our whole approach must start with the frame of reference of those to whom we would speak and not with our own. Our object is to lead others to where we are in understanding.

I try to make this point on college campuses when I speak to black student organizations. These groups have tremendous potential power, but their potential can be realized fully only through clear thinking. Thinking does not involve watering down one's convictions. On the contrary, it may permit a far pithier approach. Our objective must be to engage others so indisputably on the basis of their own principles, predispositions, and assumptions that they must either accept our position and change or abandon their principles (or be as exposed clearly hypocritical).

Such baring of issues, setting the crooked against the straight and the rough places against the smooth, is the task of prophecy. Black men who falsely advise America are no less than agents of this nation's destruction. Black men who advise white America without adequate understanding of and contact with the currents stirring the black community are like men who practice medicine without credentials. They must in some way be compelled to do their homework or be exposed as frauds who imperil the whole nation's safety.

Vincent Harding writes:

> But I think that we are beginning to see that the gift of prophecy that the black people have within America is also a gift for the world at large. We should have known this and we should have understood it before. We should have understood when that strange black genius, W. E. B. Du Bois, began speaking at the beginning of this century. We should have heard the judgment concerning present and future when he began saying in 1900, that the problem of the twentieth century would be the problem of the color line, the relation of whites to the darker races of men in Asia, in Africa, in America, and in the islands of the sea. We should have been listening then, but we weren't, and missed the reality of this gift of prophecy. We should have been listening after World War I—that marvelous war that was fought to make the world safe for democracy while 150 black Americans were being lynched each war year.

Dr. Harding then cites a passage in which Du Bois

prophesies so much of what we have seen fulfilled over the past fifty years. Du Bois spoke with irresistible logic: If two are added to two, the result will—most likely!—be four. Dr. Harding continues:

This was the black gift of prophecy as it was offered to the nation and the world in 1920, but America could not listen. It could not realize that here in the wilderness of this strange and tortuous experience known as being black in America, this man was telling the nation what was coming if it did not change its ways. It is the same gift of prophecy that we see when Martin Luther King speaks about the insane direction of American foreign policy, and we dare not try to put him back into a proscribed box called civil rights. It is the same gift of prophecy that Malcolm X was trying to practice when he spoke about "chickens" of American violence "coming home to roost" at the death of President Kennedy. Perhaps, in a frightening way, it is the closing manifestations of the gift of prophecy that James Baldwin was exercising when last year he wrote from his self-imposed exile.

Baldwin wrote:

We are in the hideous center of a mortal storm which many of us saw coming. Many of us will perish and certainly no one of my generation can hope honorably to survive . . . I am concerned with the living. I am concerned with a new morality and a new creation. I hope I do not sound literary. In any case, I mean what I say. I really believe it is possible for human beings to make the world a place in which we all can live.

Here, truly, are words of prophecy, bearing the present's

meaning for tomorrow, if there is to be one. They reflect what Vincent Harding has called the "new reality," the gift black people bring in our day.

Instruments of Peace

Vincent Harding writes:

There is much in our experience that may make it possible for us to have some sense of knowing what it means to be among the outcasts of the world, and this knowledge may well be the key to survival in today's world. Before he died, A. J. Muste said that the world was no longer divided between communists and non-communists (if it ever was) but the great division in the world is now between those nations who have never known humiliation and those who have known humiliation as a national experience for centuries. We who are black live among the leaders of the arrogant white west, but we've "been 'buked and we've been scorned," and our experience may have been for the world.

Freedom, like love and compassion, is something that can be gained only by sharing it with others. White America needs desperately to learn this lesson. But, before white America can learn it, black America must more fully develop the vision and then pass it on. Black people must come to see freedom as realizable for themselves only through aggressive striving for wholeness *for all of human life.*

Sam Anderson, leader in the new mood of black power and self-awareness, writing to the black students of America, explains: "To be black is not enough. To be bitter is not enough. And to know our magnificent black heritage is still not enough. We must become dedicated

human beings continuously questioning the roots of society." To question the roots of society is to examine
every action in the light of its consistency with human
dignity throughout the world.

Jesse Jackson, the late Martin Luther King's chief program organizer, is one of the great souls of our age. He is
an open-minded and compassionate builder for human
dignity, and he has a simple yardstick for every task that
he undertakes: Does it square with human dignity? If it
means betterment *for all humanity,* then Jesse Jackson
finds the task worth the pain and peril of attempting it.
It is this spirit that enabled him to develop Operation
Breadbasket, which has brought hope to so many on
Chicago's bleak, black South Side.

Jesse Jackson doesn't believe that his programs are a
permanent answer to anything. But he believes that his
principles are abiding ones. He speaks compassionately of
white American religion's irrelevant dealings with super-
ficialities that it calls "sins" when all the while it partici-
pates in the one great sin of violating the human life that
God has made. The renewal of American religion, he
feels, must come through the black churchmen of
America, but only as they themselves seek renewal rather
than aggrandizement or retribution. Ours has historically
been a heart of compassion. We must now exercise compassion in its broadest, deepest, and most compelling way
for black freedom and white salvation and for the peace
and prosperity of all who constitute our world.

Let us attend to these burning words from the pen of
Vincent Harding:

> Therefore, we who are black can no longer afford
> to be parochial. We cannot be American first. (In-
> deed, no Christian can be that!) Our gift, if it is our
> gift, like all of God's gifts, is for the world. Therefore,

like Malcolm, we must now speak and act for the world in the midst of the present American situation. This means that we must be acting and speaking again and again against almost everything that our national leaders identify as the American national interests in the world. For whether we like it or not, American interests are now almost consistently against the interest of the poor and the weak and the powerless all over the world. "National security" for America means universal insecurity upon the earth. This, I think, is perhaps a part of the new meaning of "Let my people go." Let my people go not from their blackness but from their bondage for American false images and American goals. Let my people go so that they may serve me. This, I think, is what it means. And when we ask how do we serve Him—or it or whatever he is, or wherever he is— then I think the answer comes, and it is this: If he really is dead, it means entering the struggle that he did not complete—the struggle for the children, the burning children, the struggle for the poor, the pressed-down poor, the struggle for the humiliated, the struggle for the weak, the struggle for all those who have paid the debt for the building of a modern society without ever gaining any of its benefits. If he is dead or if he is alive, if he lives somewhere or anywhere or here, serving him means going on in the spirit of that God-intoxicated swinger of a son who was called Jesus Christ. It means that this guy knew what he was talking about when he said that people who are filled with compassionate religious fervor have good news for the poor. They have sight to bring to the blind and they have freedom to work for —for all of the broken victims. This, I think, is the heart of our gift, a sense of what it is that men are trembling about and struggling about and seeking for, so that we are no longer trapped by those foolish cliches about communism versus "the free world."

The gift of blackness, I think, will open our eyes and clear our head. As I understand it, black men may now be called upon to lead the way to a transformed (and perhaps humiliated) America, not simply for the sake of America, but for the sake of the world. Those who are not black may wish to follow, but I suspect that the peculiar gift in this task is distinctly ours.

This message is what the Albert Cleages of Detroit and the Willie Wrights of Newark—along with the new Martin Luther Kings and thousands of other searching black souls—are trying in their own ways to do in every city of America.

What they need in order to complete their work is the compassion first and foremost of their black brothers. If what black folks call "soul"—which is another term for the "new reality"—is to be used effectively for world peace and black freedom, then black folks must relate to one another at every turn and in far more positive and mutually supportive ways than they now do.

A black administrative aide to a white business executive tells, revealingly, how he condemned a group of so-called "militants" who came into a high-level meeting of white businessmen. He says that he was embarrassed by their presence and that he gave them a tongue lashing. In retrospect, he says, their presence was his great opportunity to point out how aspects of our system are so out of joint that black people are understandably angry. He could have been supportive of the so-called "militants" and thereby gained so very much himself. We must learn that black unity must precede truly effective community, and certainly we cannot become a healing force for white

America unless we are much more related to one another as black people.

To begin at the point of black unity does not mean to end there. But without black unity we shall go precisely no where. If we are to do our crucial part to heal this nation of its sickness—a task upon which our own freedom and fulfillment depend—then it must be through our unique gift. It is the gift of blackness that will purge our own soul as it works to heal our nation and world.

What can others do about this gift of blackness? Will it be their privilege to share in it? Vincent Harding is not certain, nor am I. Dr. Harding writes: "But one thing certainly can be done and that is that all people who are not black must certainly encourage every vestige of black consciousness that they see breaking out among them. For this is a gift." He cites Frantz Fanon, who calls for recognition of a new humanity in which all human life is effectively interrelated in ways that lead to dignity. Dr. Harding then explains:

> The gift of blackness will never comprehend the gift of healing unless this broken, white-oriented, western-corrupted world seeks for healing and then enters into the healing act, enters in company with the blessed black brothers. For I think the time is now beginning when the first must be last and the last must indeed be first.
>
> If you share that recognition of the meaning of this moment, then you can really rejoice. Then you can hear Stokely and not faint. You can learn from King *and* Fanon. And then you can be men and bear up to what Ronald Fair means when he says, "God, it must be terrible not to be born black in this day and age." If you are men, truly men, and especially if you claim to be men of God, then, it will be only terrible, and not deadly, like the terror of the Almighty One. Then

you can hear such words and you can say with us, "Tell it like it is, baby, Ron, tell it like it is." In other words, Amen.

Black men must, then, become redemptive before they can be redeemed; they must seek to heal before their own broken lives may become whole; they must know and be known by one another as brothers and sisters before they can relate fully with dignity and command to others.

Martin Luther King, that prince among the princes of the earth, has begun what we must continue. He began to recall America to the fulfillment of its earliest hopes. The dream he dreamed was but the age-old American dream revealed in greater glory than our forefathers could have seen it. America represents no static hope but the fulfillment of what some day must be recognized as the most important striving of all mankind, the will for human wholeness.

Dr. King sought to share in his own way what is at least in our immediate day the gift of blackness. He looked to the day when this gift would be the universal gift and inheritance of all mankind. He sought to share the gift by instilling black group pride and self-respect, by his enlarged vision of life, by his openness to truth, by his fearless voicing of prophecy, by his inclusion of all humanity within the range of his concern, and by his conviction—restated so well by his wife Coretta—that somehow this sick nation must be healed.

To the continuation of this healing task we as black brothers and sisters must now rededicate ourselves.

CHAPTER NINE

Getting
the Pitch

"It's so difficult these days to know what to do. The white people with whom I serve on our forum committee seem to want to help. But there is a problem of knowing just how best to work together when we see that the real need is for us to have more power." These words were spoken to me on long-distance telephone from Cincinnati by Mrs. Oxley. Lately there have been many variations on this theme. Just how can white and black people best cooperate today?

The issue was raised in a different way by Lillian Kelley, the wife of a New Jersey-based attorney for a Texas oil concern. John Kelley is also a member of the Department of Urban Work of the Episcopal Diocese of Newark, the agency for which I work. Lillian, in spite of her unmistakable Texas drawl, is one of those rare individuals who comes through less as a regional type than simply a "down to earth" person. Early in January 1968 she cornered me as I was leaving my office. Pointing her finger in my face, she said: "This is not Lillian talking. This is Momma. I don't care how many other things you have to do, you had better take some time out to spell out in very simple terms what we ordinary white folks ought to be doing. Then, if black folks ought to be getting together by themselves for self-development or for anything else, you ought to let some of us white folks know what it is and why. I don't know whether interraciality is out of the picture now for a time or not, but if there are things we can legitimately be doing together, for goodness' sake, spell that out, too. Won't you?"

Lillian Kelley had given me the idea for this book. Several months later I told her that the assignment, begun on the day that it was given, was well on the way toward completion. Presumably, there were countless other people who were as eager as Mrs. Kelley. Paul Fargis and Dale Timpe, the publisher's agents, agreed. They suggested that I use as a point of departure the anticipated findings and recommendations of the President's Commission on Civil Disorders and that I bring to bear as many insights as I could from my work as principal black social-science consultant to the New Jersey Governor's Select Commission on Civil Disorders. Then both men did all within their power to ensure the earliest possible publication of this book.

Here were several good examples of how to work together. Mrs. Oxley wanted others to know how. Mrs. Kelley wanted to listen. The editor in chief and general manager of Hawthorn Books wanted to spread the message to as many others as possible. Self-interest was involved in each case, which is as it should and must be for all of us. Otherwise what we do comes through as patronizing, and much of our well-intended effort is ineffective.

New Relationships

In order for black and white Americans to work together most effectively in the days ahead, there must be some new patterns of relationship.

Margaret Mead wrote, in *The New York Times* on April 20, 1968, of the need to appreciate various options on what she termed "the road to racial irrelevance in America." With the scholarly pragmatism that has always marked her approach to troublesome issues, Mrs. Mead recognizes that racial irrelevance is a reasonable goal but that it is obviously not a present reality.

She therefore recognizes the need for black power, especially as a way out of "deprivation, poverty and despair." She writes:

> The development of political black power will inevitably involve separatism, but it must be at black, not white, initiative. If a black community wishes to bound itself, turn in on itself and gather strength to turn again and face the white community, that is right.

Concerning our over-all black-white relations at present, she observes:

> New models are needed. Today, as the country with the greatest resources, we must recognize that our situation is unique. We cannot look to other nations for solutions to emulate or failures to avoid. We can no longer work with our earlier proposed solutions. Holding out integration as the principal means —as well as the ultimate goal—has proved totally inadequate.

It must be noted that Dr. Mead does not equate "racial irrelevance" and "racial integration" as goals. Although she does not reject integration, she recognizes that it is more applicable in some situations than in others. Complete desegregation, the clearing of all barriers to opportunity,

must be a national goal. Forced mixing, beyond that inevitably involved in full desegregation, may be unduly
manipulative and so become a barrier to human growth.
Dr. Mead explains:

> Americans need not choose between integration
> and black power. In fact, there are not two but at
> least three mutually supporting means for resolving
> racial inequality within the premises of American cul-
> ture which are shared by whites and blacks: immedi-
> ate integration for those with the education to use
> their gifts; political black power in the slums of the
> inner cities; a new economic and social base in the
> rural South.
>
> The aim of integration is that race and color will
> become completely irrelevant and that each Ameri-
> can will be judged on his merits and his skills. Such
> integration is most easily accomplished in the ranks
> of statesmen and scientists, lawyers and doctors,
> poets and musicians, where the requirements of gift
> or education are highest.
>
> Simultaneously, in the ghettos of the inner city,
> black Americans are confronted by situations and
> political opportunities that faced other immigrants
> who came as strangers—uprooted, nonliterate and
> unskilled—to live in cities that had been built for and
> by earlier comers. That some of the ancestors of black
> Americans came to this country against their will
> long ago is not the issue in the North.
>
> Their immigrant predecessors—Irish, Italians, East-
> ern European Jews and others—fled poverty, oppres-
> sion and despair and crowded together in the en-
> claves of the slums. They came with hope and they
> found wretched housing, hostility and discrimination.
> They also found opportunity. Though they had to dig
> ditches and work under sweatshop conditions, when

they organized politically and made demands on the society they moved up and out.

Political Roads Are Open

The waves of rural Negro immigrants arrived, and their educationally deprived adolescent children are leaving school at a time when automation and welfare have changed this familiar scene of exploitation. Nevertheless, because the Negro immigrants have settled in, because they live crowded into defined areas, the political roads to betterment that the earlier immigrants took are still open to them also.

It is a political gambit to call this racism when done by Negroes, in contrast to earlier ethnic solidarities. Political power belongs to the organized, foreign or native, white or black, on or off welfare. Black political power, based on urban concentration, can wring from politically susceptible leadership what the ghetto needs—housing, schools, policing, credit, financing, capitalization, and a chance together to develop stiff-necked self-respect, to cultivate a sense of identity, and to conserve their own traditions.

In the old Southeast, especially in the rural areas, conditions are, of course, different. There black and white have lived together, locked within the different circumstances of their ancient immigration. Caste regulations governing close relationships, not the *de facto* segregation of the North, also have produced a state of deprivation, poverty and despair.

It may be that the South, with such a different history, can shift from the old pattern of kin and caste to a new pattern of kith and kin. Nevertheless, there must be many more new economic opportunities for the whole South, otherwise emigrants will continue to tax the resources of the cities all over the country.

All movements toward change will need national planning and financing to expedite talent search and education, to meet the demands of the residents of the inner cities, and to reorganize economic opportunity in the rural South. Supported by the entire American community as a common goal, a combination of these three efforts can lead to the creation of a society in which ancestry no longer determines where a man stands and what he can do.

The primary import of Dr. Mead's statement is that new relationships must be developed to accomplish the assumed American goal of "one society."

Black and White Caucuses

Consistent with the pressing need for black people to develop a new kind of group solidarity and with the imperative that white people seriously come to grips with a culturally rooted antiblack racism is the trend toward black caucuses and the simultaneous trend toward white caucuses to relate and to respond to them.

Working through black and white caucuses has several built-in advantages. It satisfies the necessity for corporate action by black people both in the essential task of redefining their needs and goals and in commanding or creating the resources to meet those self-determined goals. It also reflects the fact that, although solitary action in the white community by white people may be salutary and even important, the urgency and magnitude of our present situation require the full impact of combined and concerted efforts.

The use of black and white caucuses has other significant advantages. It enables a unified black community to relate and speak to a power group in the white community organized specifically to hear a black message and to facilitate enlightened and substantial change.

Perhaps the greatest advantage of relationships between white and black caucuses is that both the immediate and the long-term implications of black power may best be dealt with in this way. In immediate practical terms black people need to develop group pride and purpose in order to relate most effectively to the white community. But the initial black group-oriented thinking about black power should be extended, and universalized by continual interchange with thoughtful white groups representing the greatest competence and willingness to extend their present perceptions of reality.

Inherent in the concept of black power are the most helpful clues offered in many generations to help practically every institution in our society to restructure itself to perform its function most effectively. Our educators and social workers, for example, to be effective, need in the most urgent way to deal with the issues of self-awareness and power for self-directed growth as these issues relate to their work. Black and white caucuses can very well relate to each other in spelling out implications for nurturing the nation's youth and for rehabilitating those who live largely unself-directed lives. Betty Goldsmith and Joseph McDonald of the Family Service Association in Cincinnati introduced their staff to the concept of black power as the key to "a significant break-through in social work theory and practice." A growing number of schools of social work, education, planning and architecture, law, and the other arts and sciences have begun explorations of black power as potentially the most creative social concept advanced in recent times.

To such social tasks black people must bring the perspectives of their unique cultural and historical experience. Only as black people synthesize their own rich and variegated experience can they best share the message

with others. Black people must sharpen their thoughts in
contact with one another in order to carry forward a
process of learning that our times greatly require.

Emily Moore of the New York chapter of the National
Organization of Women holds that black power must be
understood by white women as they seek greater freedom.
"Black people," she says, "can be our best ally." Dr. Jean
Simmons, President of the New Jersey Association of University Women, agrees: "To the extent that any arbitrary
standards are placed on opportunity for any in our society
all suffer. Those of us who find ourselves the principal
victims of this injustice must see our cause in common."
Barbara Sykes-Wright, who has played a prominent part
in efforts to repeal New York's abortion law, writes: "All
those who would work for the civilizing of our society
must see their cause as one with that of black people.
Mutual self-interest will require our working together."

Caucuses meet separately at times and together at other
times. They provide a structured means for retreat and
confrontation so greatly needed in many areas of our
common life. Thoughtful Americans in business, in politics, in religion, and in other areas of our civic life can
only profit from examining both their principles and their
programs in terms of how they promote the worthiest
vision of human life and encourage the fulfillment of that
vision in each individual human life.

Perhaps the most salutary aspect of American religious
life today is the work being undertaken by black churchmen in the interests of Christian renewal. "The white
churches," says Newark's Dr. Ulysses Blakeley, "can find
their salvation in the work which black churchmen presently are the best equipped by historical and cultural
circumstance to do." Black churchmen who are most in
tune with the new mood are being encouraged to organize.

Alex Poinsette of *Ebony* points out that the white churches of America have much to be grateful for, particularly in the work of Hayward Henry, leader of the Black Unitarian Caucus. Mr. Henry is a man of gentle spirit and burning conviction, who recognizes that to care enough involves a willingness to die daily death of isolation and misunderstanding. Because of his quiet determination, the black Unitarians have organized far more effectively than have the black churchmen of any other denomination. The great failure, in the estimate of some black Unitarians, is among concerned white Unitarians, who believe that individual white acquiescence is enough.

Quinton Primo, a leader of the Episcopal Church's Union of Black Clergy and Laymen, laments that white churchmen have not yet learned to deal with black men and women as their leaders, let alone as their teachers. "The theological tasks facing the Church," says Dr. Bryant George of the United Presbyterian Church's national staff, "call for 'ears to hear' and 'eyes to see' on the part of white Christians. Our hope is that they will awaken in sufficient time to be saved."

"Our white-controlled churches," says Episcopal Bishop John Burgess, "must create new means for hearing and heeding black people. Especially must some means be created 'post haste' for the unfolding of the essential theological dimensions which black minds may offer the Church, especially in our troubled times."

Father Louis Burrell, a member of the remarkably large caucus of black Roman Catholic priests, speaks of the need for his church to grow into a new maturity and openness to reality: "Due to the paternalistic attitude of the church, I don't think my parishioners would even tell me if they thought Stokely Carmichael had something to say."

Black churches too are slowly beginning to rediscover

the meaning of being black. As powerful instruments representing the black community's present aspirations, Reverend Kelsey Jones of the Christian-Methodist-Episcopal Church suggests, their resurgence can do perhaps more than any other single agency to prepare white churchmen to relate in equitable ways to their brother black American churchmen.

The black and white caucuses at the Colgate Rochester Divinity School, formed in the fall of 1967, worked together so well that the administration decided in the early spring of 1968 to establish a department of black studies. Initially a black professor would be engaged to assist the entire school in reviewing its life through insights afforded by black power in its broadest dimensions. Bobby Joe Saucer, founder of the Colgate Rochester black caucus, reports that the black students have grown immeasurably in their sense of self-worth as they see themselves more as benefactors of the school than as "guests" and recipients of white bounty, as they previously had done. The white students by and large are elated. They have discovered that many changes they had hoped for are now possible through the new relationships with the black student body.

Largely instrumental in encouraging the caucus concept at the Colgate Rochester Divinity School was Professor Prentiss Pemberton, to whom the black students, during a brief period of anger and rebellion in the spring of 1967, turned for aid in interpreting to the school their sense of isolation and of alienation. The school's president, Dr. Gene Bartlett, has suggested that open and frank dealing with this frustration has enabled the school to accept realities and to begin to come to terms with problems in far more substantial and creative ways. "We are grateful," says Dr. Bartlett, "that these black students have begun to help us in new ways."

Teaching and Learning

Those who are white and who would hear new truths from black people must be humble enough to listen and also concerned enough to encourage black people to sharpen their thinking constantly. John McClaughry, a former special assistant to Senator Charles Percy, quickly came to see the concept of black power as fundamentally related to broad needs in our society. He has therefore worked diligently to gain consideration of it among as many legislators as possible, stressing its implications for many areas of their work not immediately related to the needs of black people. His use of the insights of black power were crucial in the brilliant research for and preparation of the brief for the Percy-sponsored Home Ownership Foundation Act.

John McClaughry's easy and helpful candor, as well as his eagerness to ensure the most productive employment of black men's talents for peace and progress in our society, are reflected in a letter he wrote to a black associate. It reads in part:

It is a little presumptuous of a white country boy to tell a black ghetto man what it is that he should want. That is what I am about to do, so I hope you will also forgive this presumption.

There are many good points in your Confrontation paper, but basically, I don't think you know what you really want or how to get it. What you really want, I think, is *the power* and *the means* to build the kind of community your people want and deserve to have, and the sole right to benefit from the profits that result. You not only should want better homes, but also to own those homes. You not only should want decent food in the supermarket, but ownership of that super-market. You should want not only a respectful audience from Congress, but the clout to make Congress move. You should want not only increased economic viability in the ghetto, but also that the profits from the ghetto to stay and work in the ghetto.

So you come to Congress and ask for $6 billion in public housing. Who is going to make a profit from the sale of the land? Not Negroes. The demolition contract? Not Negroes. The construction? Not the Black People's Construction Company, because there isn't one. The labor wages? Not Negroes—laborers, maybe, not electricians and plumbers, who really make the bread. And when it is ready for occupancy, who is the new landlord? Not Negroes. The New York Public Housing Authority. This all presumes Congress would lay out another $6 billion for public housing. I can tell you it will lay out $6 billion for riot control before it lays out $6 billion for public housing. So what is to be done?

You need to confront Congress, all right, but in a sophisticated way that uses other people's wrong impulses for leverage, just as judo uses the opponent's momentum against him. You have got to design a program that allies your goals with those of others who will go along with what you want.

Here, off the top of my head, are some thoughts.

1. Where does financing come from? Banks and savings and loans. Who owns them? White people. *Item 1:* Government aid in creating and strengthening black financial institutions. How? Maybe by depositing Federal funds in ghetto banks. Maybe by amending the Federal Savings and Loan Insurance Act to double the insurance maximums in S & Ls that make ghetto loans.

2. Who owns the present buildings? White people. *Item 2:* Identify ownership of buildings with code violations and hit them so hard they have to sell out cheap to Negroes to escape the penalty. How? Terrific fines for code violations. Liberal tax deductions for selling to neighborhood organizations at rock-bottom prices. Reduction of depreciation allowances by a multiple of building code fines assessed. Receivership for failure to make repairs. Neighborhood-based courts with elected judges to hear housing cases.

3. Who gets the building or rehabilitation contracts? White companies. *Item 3:* Government aid to encourage the formation of broadly owned black construction companies big enough to take on big jobs and make big money. How? Amending Subchapter S of the Revenue Code to permit flow-through of corporate profits. Paid full-time managers until qualified Negroes can take over. Army Corps of Engineers officers on free loan. Long-term, low-cost loan insurance. Tax deductibility of equipment or salaries donated by private business.

4. Who gets the wages? White building tradesmen. *Item 4:* Get Negroes into building trades unions. How? Intensive training programs to enable low-skill Negroes to qualify. Formation of a "rehabilitation mechanics brotherhood" within the Building and Construction Trades Council; if they won't go along, go to District 50 of the United Mine Workers, or the Teamsters. Cut across jurisdictional lines at the bottom. Picket white building jobs until they get the word.

5. Who owns the buildings? The government. *Item 5:* Cooperative or condominium ownership by the people themselves, without loss of subsidization.

6. Where are jobs created? Big companies lo-

cating in the ghetto. Who makes the profits? White people. *Item 6:* Government inducement to companies to sell stock equal to the value of the project to the people in the neighborhood, and government-insured loans to enable them to buy it.

Now these are just a few things just off the top of my head; I don't profess to have thought them all the way through. But they may be suggestive. To them I would add neighborhood control of schools (as recommended by the Bundy report) and tax resources . . .

The bill would simply have provided the device for tapping the capital market and putting the proceeds at the disposal of neighborhood housing sponsors, and it would have given poor people a subsidy to make the mortgage payments on their homes or apartments. What is so damned complicated about that? It didn't answer every problem of the ghetto, but it would have *put buying power in the hands of neighborhood organizations* seeking better housing, and it would have transferred the ownership of housing to the poor people themselves. And it was so designed to minimize the demands on the Federal Treasury by using a powerful leverage effect on the private sector. I should point out to you that your $2 billion in FNMA takeout money for 221(d)(3) mortgages will get you just 20,000 $10,000 units. The $60 *million a year* in the Percy bill would have gotten you 200,000 $10,000 units. That is because the $60 million is payable every year for 30 years, while the $2 billion initial outlay under the FNMA system begins to repay the second year. But the important thing is that Congress may vote $60 million in *this* deficit budget (and let succeeding Congresses worry about continuing the payments) but it will *not* vote any $2 billion in this deficit budget of $29 or $35 billion.

Unfortunately, confused people couldn't understand this; and thus the Johnson Administration was able to scuttle this in favor of a good old tried and true [sic] FHA program, which will work if (a) FHA will insure where it has never done so before, (b) banks will put up the funds where they have never done so before, even with insurance, (c) the President authorizes FNMA to buy the mortgages, and (d) FNMA actually buys the mortgages at par. If you think this sort of "existing program" will work, you get out this letter two years from now and read it again.

You are right to put the finger on your urban Congressmen and to mass your political muscle. Where you are wrong is insisting that they support fantastic demands which they can't put across. Get yourself a sophisticated program, including both legislative and executive action, that makes sense, then put on the screws. There's nothing like opposition to make Congressmen get scared. If you are going to stay Democrats—on the plantation, in my opinion—form independent Democrat councils and run primary opponents where necessary. Better yet, take over the Republican organization and force the Republican Party to give full support to your efforts. I am convinced that conservative business-oriented Republicans will support your demands for economic power *if it is explained to them in their own language.* Witness Dr. Mathews' experience with the Queens Conservative Party. . . .

You can dramatize moral issues by marches on Washington like that of 1963 (I was there), but when it gets down to economic matters, which is the real guts of the Negro's plight, there is a whole interest-group structure to be manipulated. He who knows how to make it move in his direction gets what he

wants. He that confronts it with a list of demands will
go home very unhappy—probably unhappy enough
to start a "disturbance."

Now I have said all this straight from the shoulder.
I really feel strongly that the black man has got to
have power to control his environment. But right and
indignation is no substitute for sophistication and
knowledge, and that is what this movement has got to
have . . . If you don't get it from somewhere, you are
going to be turned down, then riot, and then alienate
the people whose support you have to have and can
get if you do it right . . .

Don't get me wrong—I am 105% for the goals you
seek. I just don't want to see you embark on a counter-
productive effort which will only result in mutual ill
will and heightened frustration. I wish I could take 2
or 3 years to help put your program across, but I can't;
and besides, you need a black general leading the
army. I'd like to do what I can from time to time,
however, and I hope you will feel free to call on me.

Here is forthright help, unmarked by the kind of paternalism and arrogance that for far too long have characterized white America's dealings with black America.

A precondition for working effectively in unity in the
days ahead will be the willingness of white Americans to
take a far different attitude toward black people than they
have taken in the past. It calls for not much more than a
sincere and conscious effort to be genuinely human, to put
aside the mask of pretense that whiteness in America inevitably tends to involve. This requirement places a much
greater burden on black people. It means willingness to
convert much of our understandable anger into patient
concern and thoughtful and open dealing with issues
despite repeated misunderstanding; and it requires, above

all else, a willingness to grow in the same way that we would wish white America to do.

Toward a New Vocabulary

Language often proves to be a significant *barrier* to communication, especially in current efforts of black and white people to work together for the nation's peace.

"Law and Order"

Some white groups and individuals express willingness to work with black people if only it can be fully understood that first and foremost we must have "law and order." "Law and order" means different things to different people. V. L. Parrington, in *Main Currents in American Thought,* describes the thought of the Virginia Republican philosopher John Taylor (1753–1824):

> In his analysis of the origins of government, he discovers in every society a master class that becomes the beneficiary of sovereign power; the political state is first erected and thereafter used to safeguard the past acquisitions and to further the present ambitions of a dominant economic group which calls itself an aristocracy; and such an aristocracy imposes its will upon the exploited mass, crudely by the sword and purse, and subtly by the skillful use of psychology. Once in control of the political state it intrenches itself behind certain fictions which profess to carry moral sanction. This political jugglery plays many tricks to catch the gullible; arrayed in the garb of patriotism, loyalty, obedience to authority, law and order, divine right, it carries a weighty appeal. When

these moral fictions fail, the fictions of the law step in, and such doctrines as the sacredness of contract translate the stealings of the master class into vested interests which the state is bound to protect. (Vol. II, p. 15)

The poor and the excluded in every society, finding that the social order does not serve their basic needs, do not see that order as legitimate. Only as a society grants substantial equity to all does it have legitimacy in the minds of all. Those who are excluded from reasonable benefit levels and from participation in equitable power relations experience what others call "law and order" only as repression.

In our own day, there is the most urgent need to redefine "law and order" to allow for the rapid but orderly change and progress demanded by a continuously changing and growing technology. Thinking conservatives are always most sensitive to the need for change. They recognize that precipitate revolution is inefficient, to say the least, in that it wantonly destroys much that is good as it clears the landscape for reform. Yet human life does not long endure oppression. Those who are wise know it, and those who are both responsible and wise will always work to adjust the best that the past has bequeathed to the best that the future promises.

Reaction always reflects the grossest irresponsibility in its arrogant and foolhardy risking of the good that past generations have created and preserved for posterity. Our present abandonment of discretion is evinced both in our mounting national insensitivity to the *urgency* of the already long-unanswered need for equality for all and in our brutal restort to uncivilized public massacres in the name of law and order.

A society that is not fundamentally humane is not civilized. We should not forget that it is not "due process" but reverence for human life and the will toward life that distinguish civilization.

Those who represent the forces of entrenched and unequal power tend always to lose perspective. It seems elementary to assume in this light that white America, with its long-entrenched and unjust hold on the reins of power, has become astigmatic in its vision of reality and also callous and wanting in reverence for human life.

In terms of our present efforts at communication and cooperation between white and black people, black people increasingly are finding a tremendous barrier in the failure of white Americans to be humble enough to see themselves—even theoretically—as representing an order or system that, in its nature, tends to be inhumane.

On the other hand, those who raise the alarm when things go wrong must be recognized as both heroic and responsible. We applaud the man who, upon seeing a fire, sounds the alarm and saves both life and property. Yet in the far more important area of human relations, where lives are daily maimed, stunted, and destroyed, those who sound the alarm are ignored. Then, when their anguished cries for simple attention to human dignity remain unanswered and they commit acts of desperation, we call their voices "discordant" and for their acts bring them before the bar of judgment. How easy it is to move unconsciously from righteousness to arrogance! We all tend to do it, and we must forever be on guard lest our defense of what we see as good works in subtle ways to destroy the dignity of others.

In my own household, the single most civilizing force has been our oldest son, David, who is now a naval petty officer. On several occasions in his high-school years, he challenged our unknowing arrogance with stubborn dignity. The family, fortunately, at last caught on, and every good to which we have since committed our lives has been shaped in the direction of greater reverence for human life largely because of what our son David did *for us.*

Those who put "law and order" first must come to see that reverence for human dignity as an end in human life takes precendence over "due process," which is only a means. The two concerns must be kept in balance, but there must be no doubt of which is the greater.

Joseph Leidy, a young investment broker in the affluent and conservative community of Morristown, New Jersey, spoke recently of his earnest hopes that those who called themselves responsible men would cease equating a kind of lofty indifference with "responsibility." The lofty indifference of able people may be no less than our Achilles' heel, he felt. Responsible men, women, and young people are those whose behavior is appropriate to the needs and circumstances of each changing and advancing hour.

"Then Change Things at the Polls!"

Those who assume that black people are negligent in their use of the polls to achieve change—or that they fail to take advantage of the same opportunities that have served others—raise barriers to cooperation and communication.

Aside from the deliberate crushing of the wills of black men, the unconscious grooves that our systematic racism has created build in limitations that we have not consciously willed or even recognized. Our well-intended provision of sanitary housing for black people, for example, has done incalculable harm by effectively undermining their power of civic participation. Urban renewal has deracinated black people.

"Deracination" is the technical term for rendering people rootless. The process has a number of weakening effects. Urban renewal—and its updated version, the so-called "Model Cities program"—has tended to make black people feel that they *do not belong* in any one place. People who are constantly moved about tend to share the outlook or psychology of outsiders in relation to the civic and social life in which others participate. They tend not to reregister repeatedly to vote. They tend to take less responsibility for local order, safety, cleanliness, and improvement. They invest less in learning and in working. Life in general has a tenuous nature for them, and human relations, though possibly warm, are not developed in depth. The "maximum local involvement" provision in the Model Cities legislation does not provide an antidote to the long-standing, built-in rootlessness of large segments of the black community.

We cannot afford to continue to manipulate human life in such a way as to further the subtly corrosive process of deracination. This fact is of the greatest urgency, for growing population movement is certain to increase rootlessness. Those who wish to preserve the democratic political system must work now to halt the pernicious effects of the serious and increasing rootlessness that our seemingly well-intentioned government housing policies have served to aggravate, in the black community especially.

Those who assume, with the greatest good will, that the provisions of "adequate" new or more sanitary housing is even an issue unconsciously overlook the pernicious effects of "forced moving" in itself. Black people particularly cannot afford to be shaped by arbitrary circumstance into "outsiders" in our society. Forced moving must always be compensated for. The nation, indeed, would do well—and save money over even a decade—in "compensating" black people in part as an act of restitution, with massive aid to encourage home ownership. All new housing for black people should be ownership housing. Such a provision would pay for itself by its positive effects on the maintenance of our domestic urban peace. The

repeated tragic waste of several previous long, hot sum-
mers should be anticipated and prevented by the use of
funds for providing equity in the nation's life for black
people—funds at least equivalent to those spent in controlling or cleaning up after the riots.

Similarly, black adults who have been uprooted from
the soil that might have supported past community growth
should be given the same second chance for maximum
productivity as is being afforded black veterans in accelerated teacher-training preparation in St. Louis County,
Missouri. There is every good reason for large numbers of
black urban adults to receive college training for teaching
and also engineering and construction, at least to the
associate-degree level. Two of our most immediate fore-
seeable employment needs are for capable and concerned
urban teachers of black youth and for men to build in
thirty years enough housing to match all the housing previously built in the nation's history. Black people can—
with forthright and honest governmental action—easily
be afforded a fair role in the building trades, and urban
education can and should be a primary source of employment and justice for black people.

Those who would work with black people must see how
past good intentions have blocked or subverted the demo-
catic process and imperiled the nation's orderly, peaceable,
and efficient progress. Costly relief programs are not the
fundamental answer. Far more than material bounty, people need the capacity to participate effectively in deciding
their own needs and the power to command the resources
to meet these needs. A responsible look at our mistakes
and prompt use of the natural opportunities for their
permanent correction that lie ahead are what we most
require.

Black and white Americans must face this need together. We must work together to assure equitable investment for all in a society characterized by a growing

rootlessness that, if allowed to continue, may undermine the political and economic foundations of our nation. The rootless, the deracinated, not only do not vote, but also they tend to become isolated, alienated—reflecting the failure of society to function reasonably for the good of all—and thus dangerous.

"We're Doing Our Best!"

The attitude among white people who exclaim "But we are really doing our best!" also creates a barrier to common work with black people. They are saying in effect: "Don't tell us that we are doing anything that isn't right or that we ought to change in any way! But let's somehow work together."

This attitude has come to the fore especially since the recent reports on civil disorders. White America, in its defensiveness, has raised new barriers to creative relationships. Openness to change and to honest confrontation of issues must always be a precondition for harmonious working with others.

A promising exception to this negative attitude was expressed in the spring of 1968 by Minnesota's Commissioner for Human Rights, Frank Kent, an able black man. He speaks with the authority of his 97 per cent white state behind him. "Our state," he wrote to me, "wants to make a model state response to the implications of the recent civil disorders reports. We want to take the lead, pointing the way for the peace and progress of the nation." He added, "Knowing of your passionate concern for those who think of themselves as responsible conservatives to take the lead in being responsible we felt that you might be in a position to help us in some way as our 'responsibly conservative' state tries to fulfill its trust for human rights."

After a brief telephone conversation in which we agreed that satisfying the urgent needs of the most benighted people in our cities is of a piece with the self-interest of all America, Commissioner Kent then asked that I provide advisory help in Minnesota's pioneering effort for urban peace.

Specifically, I was requested to draft a proposal for a week-end orientation session for members of the Minnesota Advisory Board on Human Rights and the members of the Commission's own professional staff. The agenda agreed upon included the implications of black power as a creative social concept, applicable by extension to the needs of all; antiblack racism (as part of the American cultural value system shared by white and black alike); and the psychology of revolt as a built-in warning that all is not well in present patterns of institutional life. We also agreed that possibly some key state personnel should be included in the week-end orientation session, which was to involve no more than fifty people.

As staff preparation, the following preliminary questionnaire was prepared. The staff was asked to review and to refine it.

Preliminary Questionnaire for the Consultation on Urban Crisis

1. *Housing*

    a) Number and types of new housing in the state. (By year: 1956–1967)
    b) What new housing is ownership housing?
    c) What new housing is rentership housing?
    d) What is the breakdown for a, b, and c above by race?
    e) What open housing policies exist in the state?
    f) What types—and names—of communities "zone out" housing under $15,000? Under $12,000?

g) What new housing plans are afoot?

h) What specifically is being done to stop rentership for minorities and to aggressively encourage home ownership?

i) What are major stumbling blocks? Major opportunities?

j) How have urban renewal programs affected voting patterns?

k) What is the history of urban renewal? Indicate by year in terms of both actual construction and the designation of tracts for clearance, etc.

2. *Employment*

a) What are the percentages and numbers of employed and unemployed by race in the state? In the major urban areas?

b) Translate a into a ten-year chart from 1957–1967.

c) What percentage and numbers of minority group migrants have come to the state—and where—over a ten-year period?

d) What is the history of state and federal economic opportunity aid? By types of programs? By year? By dollar amounts? By percentage increases and decreases? By employment patterns as to race, including salary ranges and decision-making status?

e) What criteria have been used for success? What are figures and percentages of below-poverty-level people by year since OEO aid and programming? How has OEO affected the relief picture in the state? In urban areas?

f) How has early retirement affected the job picture?

g) What percentages and numbers of jobs in spe-

cific communities and by specific categories
must minority people be facilitated into in
order to make actual rather than implied
"progress" in employment updating for minorities? Have timetables and specific year-by-year
goals and procedures (which may be critiqued
for success or failure) for securing equity in
employment for minorities? Under whose auspices? In what communities?

h) How do state and municipal governments and
   public education institutions stand up under g?

i) Have any efforts been made to scrap "equal"
   opportunity in favor of "equitable" opportunity
   (in the spirit of "equity and restitution" procedures)?

j) What are examples of the best employment
   patterns by industry? Support the cases factu-
   ally using criteria from above questions.

k) What seem to be major stumbling blocks in
   this area? What are major opportunities?

3. *Education*

a) What major changes have been made in the
   educational program for the state to reflect
   precipitous changes in our society since World
   War II?

b) What is the history of drop-outs since World
   War II? For the state? By urban or rural area?
   By race?

c) What is the relationship between urban and
   rural state aid? Translate into dollar figures
   and percentages by year since 1945.

d) What specific programs have been instituted
   for recruitment of minority group teachers in
   particular? Give details.

e) What specific programs have been designed

for urban education? By whom were they designed? What criteria were used in the designs? What criteria were used in the selection of designers?

f) What plans for educational re-entry have been made for "drop-outs"?

g) What plans are made for continuing education of *all* adults, especially those under $8,000/yr.?

h) What re-training programs have been developed or projected? What "success" have they had? How many people needed to be reached? How many were reached? How many secured jobs? How long did they keep them?

i) What are numbers and percentages of black students and teachers in public schools? In higher education? (Please chart from 1957 to 1967.)

j) Since "urban" problems are most urgent in educational planning, how many black officials are there in the following categories:
   —state boards of education
   —state institutional wards (where youth live in)
   —municipal and county boards of education
   —institutional directorships
   —municipal or county superintendencies and assistant superintendencies
   —central office supervisory roles

k) What plans have been made to acquire these resources?

l) What seem to be major stumbling blocks in education? Major opportunities?

4. *Public Services*

a) What plans and procedures for *equitable* employment are there for state and local public services, including partial moratoria on majority group hiring and upgrading, etc.?

b) What plans have been made to review in depth the status, job descriptions, and hence also the pay of the officers of the peace to make these commensurate with our increasingly sophisticated society?

c) Has the state made any moves to professionalize the roles of officers of the peace by requiring graduate school training in the future and using available funds for academic re-training for present officers?

d) What plans have been made to change roles and images of officers of the peace from that of seeming aggressors to positive advocacy, as suggested by the civil disorders reports?

5. *Public Accommodations*

a) What are the problems and opportunities in this area?

b) Are there laws limiting teenage youth from employment?

c) If public transportation is under this category, how does this affect minority group employment opportunities?

When the staff reviewed the questionnaire, there was agreement that implicit in the questions themselves was a program for human rights for some years to come. What are some of the program needs suggested by the questionnaire to which commissions on human relations and other formal and informal groups of black and white people working together might address themselves?

Housing. The underlying issue raised by the questions

on housing is that of control *by all our citizens* of their immediate environments.

The issue of what housing is provided for what people and why is as important for the nation's future today as the issue of conservation was in Theodore Roosevelt's time. Because of the projected needs for home building in the next thirty years, the nation as a whole—and every individual community—has an unprecedented opportunity to plan in such a way as to compensate for past mistakes and to make future communities more nearly ideal.

All housing must come to be fully desegrated, as nonexclusive communities with common interests thus have the opportunity to grow. All zoning laws must be reviewed with the largest public interest in view. Large communities that "zone out" lower-priced housing units effectively restrict entry by religious and ethnic groups that may be concentrated in lower-income occupations. The key question might be How can our goal of "one society" and the nation's internal peace be achieved by this unique opportunity to plan for anticipated massive housing needs?

So many of our present urban problems have come about because of precipitate, unplanned metropolitan-area change since World War II. How it happened and the results are the principal thesis developed in my *Ready To Riot*. Planning for housing must take into consideration the need for self-directed growth and for self-respect for everyone. All housing must be designed as settings in which human beings can best realize their potential. It must be planned as much as possible by those who will occupy it, who should also own and manage it. It is a monumental task, but, for the safety and survival of all, we must confront it together.

Employment. With increased automation and early retirement, the nation's employment patterns will change. Those who are most interested in nonrevolutionary change have now—if they begin quickly—the chance of a lifetime to build equity for all into an economic system that may still preserve a substantial measure of freedom.

The director of admissions of one of the great institutions of higher learning tells how he suddenly became aware of the kinds of steel walls of prejudice and restricted opportunity that men are unmindfully building. He says that throughout his life he had never had the experience of belonging to a rejected minority. Then in middle life he became a member of the nonacademic minority among university personnel. He was instantly an outsider, and for months he was filled with unvented rage. Then fortunately he found in one of his black associates an able counselor who helped him to recognize his situation as one of rejected-minority status. This director of admissions admitted that, although he knows that his situation was not exactly like that of black people, he felt for once the reality of walls that even men of good will have unknowingly built and sincerely claim are not there.

Those who are concerned with our persistent inability to mobilize fully the talent of this nation not only for justice and peace but also for the far greater enrichment of our common life must come to terms with the subtle effects of our culturally determined blind spots. Why are there so few trained black people in administrative posts in our educational, governmental, and business life? Why is the major economic problem for black people underemployment rather than unemployment? Underemployment suggests arbitrary and unreasonable waste. Can the nation afford to continue to ignore available talent?

"Made" work must not be allowed to become a substitute for productive work for our black urban minority as long as productive tasks remain to be done for the common good. Nor should we continue to mislead ourselves that we are eliminating poverty or creating "fair employment" when experience shows that our programs and practices are not fulfilling our intentions. Apprenticeship programs—which provide the most economical means for craft education—should be reviewed both to reveal their present failures and to discover creative possibilities for adjusting all adult education toward the associate or bachelor's degree. Must journeymen be "outsiders" in the process of liberating education? These men vote and become leaders. They should be equipped for the tasks of civic life that they inevitably are called upon to fulfill.

In every community, state, and region of the nation, employment practices must be examined to determine precisely how the economic gap between black and white Americans can be closed. New mechanisms to ensure permanent employment opportunity for all must be created. Nowhere has it been done so far.

Education. The black "drop out" rate represents the critical human problem in education. What we do to black people is only an indication of what we do to all the defenseless in our society.

We must understand the companionship in alienation currently being experienced by black students and some white dissident groups in our colleges. Pervasive and long-standing needs, made more apparent by growing self-awareness among black students, are simply underscored by the sometimes raucous protests of white students. The black students at Columbia University have long protested the unreality in their American history and other courses. But, before the protest in the spring of 1968, they could achieve no hearing. The same is true of almost any other white or white-directed American university, and the failure of response would probably be the same. What is happening, unfortunately, in too much of our educational structure is that the curriculum, rather than the students' changing needs for growth, has been the assumed beginning and end of education.

Education today, thanks to the focus on human dignity

brought about chiefly by black people, has the opportunity to reshape its goals with more emphasis on the
humane—or to bog down in painful waste.

Our entire educational enterprise—from the cradle to
the grave—must be humanized, starting with the need for
human wholeness and ending as close as possible to the
fulfillment of that need. Education must be for living, and
the process must last all life long. Continuing education
in vocational and avocational skills for everyone from
eighteen to eighty must be established thoughout the
nation. Our changing patterns of work and recreation, as
well as the need for men to live in company with the best
that all the ages afford, call for no less.

Traditional higher education, however notable its efforts, is not keeping up with the changing needs of the
times, nor has it apparently even heard the call to enrich
life for all who are past adolescence. "Higher" education
must become "adult" and "continuing" education. The
term "elite" in our society must come to indicate the basic
capabilities in every man, in which each may be encouraged to excel.

In a nation in which men move about freely, national
priorities and subsidies seem to be the only reasonable
way to attain excellence for all in our educational enterprise. The educational needs of black youth and adults
may provide us with a basis for seeing more clearly the
educational needs of all. We must understand these needs,
and we must work together to devise new—and efficient,
enduring, and economical—solutions for all.

Public services and accommodations. The concern for
humanity of a state and of any community is evidenced by
the equitable way in which it provides its public services
and affords hospitality and sanctuary to those who are its
guests.

The public for far too long has complained of undue
casualness on the part of public servants, as epitomized by

the proverbial slowness of some postal clerks to respond to customers awaiting service. There is never an excuse for an officer of the peace to raise his voice to citizens. His job can and must be performed with courtesy and efficiency. Public servants—in every department of government and at every level—must come to see themselves as servants of the public and not as its masters. There is no single more demoralizing factor in our society than the growing lack of a sense of service among those called upon to serve the public needs. Here also is a key to the problem of disrespect for law and lack of confidence in the processes of government. Public servants may—and must —be called upon to set the tone necessary to check mounting national cynicism.

The need for adequate and equitable public services will be more pronounced as the nation grows. Tourism can become a major part of our future national economic life if our people learn the art of public *service* and public hospitality. The scriptural injunction, "Give and it shall be given in return to you, full measure, pressed down and running over," can result in a social, economic, and civic reality if, in our public services and accommodations, we learn service and fair play. We cannot improve as we must to create such a future unless first unmet present needs, especially in regard to our minorities, are fulfilled. Doing unto others as we would have them do unto us can more than guarantee ethical behavior. It can assure peace, progress, and prosperity for all. We can and must work together to bring this condition to pass.

Language and attitudes that reflect simple resignation are barriers to communication. Governor Levander of Minnesota and his cabinet officers and staff are, by their openness and willingness to seek new possibilities for urban peace, blazing a path on which other states and communities can follow.

"But I Couldn't Cooperate With Him!"

Whoever "him" may be, unless Americans can see their own self-interest in working with one another, the nation's future is in peril. Either our fortunes are interrelated, or we are not "one nation, under God, indivisible."

Black people must work together within the nation. Their unity is necessary for the development of equitable power relations with others who constitute America. In the broadest sense, we must all come to see that our best interests are served only as our individual and group interests correspond most closely with those of the nation as a whole.

Perhaps the most serious problem in this regard is in our use of language and in our dismissive labeling of others. When "radicals" yell like hell, the noise should alert thoughtful "conservatives" to the possibility that in some way all that they are conserving may not be just right. In our homes we sometimes have sufficient sensitivity to those close to us to realize that alien behavior may be the direct result of our own unconscious alienating acts. Those who would overcome others' alienation must adjust both their speech and their hearing to make communication possible.

Senator Charles Percy writes:

> We must work to create a working alliance between conservatives and the people of the ghettos. For, in truth, they are saying the same things, but each in language only slightly comprehensible to the other. I am convinced that if the way could be found to convert the language of the Country Club into the language of Kedzie and Roosevelt Road, and vice versa, conservatives and militant slum dwellers alike would realize their common interests and begin to work together for their common goals: individual

liberty, equal opportunity, independence, local initiative and responsibility. (*The Congressional Record,* December 6, 1967)

That all Americans must come to see urban peace and
fulfillment for black people as in their own interests should
be elementary, as tensions mount. We can no longer afford the luxury of failing to synthesize and to modify our
perceived self-interests so that our own good is a fundamental part of the good of all. Between liberals and conservatives and between black and white men there may
be tensions, but there must always be creative interchange
as well.

The fundamental benefit from overcoming barriers in
working relations between black and white Americans
today may be growth in our capacity to understand
"America first" in a new light, one in which our own needs
are always related to the needs of all.

CHAPTER TEN

Urgent
Responsibilities

IN A TIME OF GREAT CRISIS OVER THE PLACE OF BLACK MEN
in American life Thomas Jefferson wrote, "I tremble for
my country when I remember that God is just, that his
justice cannot sleep forever."

This sleeping justice even today threatens to rend our
nation. Although we accept the truism that justice too
long delayed is not justice at all, we frequently forget that
a society in which gross injustice prevails makes all men
who willingly participate in it unjust. For our own health
and preservation as a people, then, we must work together
to ensure that the justice inherent in nature, as Mr. Jefferson might put it, does not bring our national experiment
to a swift and painful end.

Essential Communication

In order for black men and white men to work together to bring peace and fulfillment to this nation, there
must be communication between them.

That important communication already exists at various levels must not be overlooked. We must, as a matter of simple efficiency, see what relationships already exist, and then we must build upon the foundations that are there. We can find no better existing interracial mechanisms to build upon and extend than those afforded by such "old line" organizations as the National Association for the Advancement of Colored People, its Legal Defense Fund, the National Urban League, and the Congress of Racial Equality. Fair-housing associations and various interracial religious, business, labor, educational, and civic groups at national and local levels also provide substantial opportunities for work across racial lines toward making our communities and our nation approximate our ideals for them.

But there is an urgency in our times that makes our situation precarious. Massive and immediate efforts should therefore be made to extend interracial work both as a supplement and as a catalyst for other activity that can best be accomplished only *within* ethnic groups. Indeed, we cannot learn precisely what we should do within our own ethnic groups unless there is interracial communication. Existing organizations must therefore be encouraged. The white-dominated Urban Coalition, about which many black men have grave reservations because of its orientation toward physical planning, must also be recognized as having a place. In interracial activity related to urban matters and in all our specifically black affairs, black men should for some time provide the strategic leadership. In fact, there can be no substantial change in the critical area of power relations unless a similar change first takes place in the white-dominated agencies that strive to facilitate change. White leadership can serve best, in our immediate situation, within the structures of the white community itself. Simple economy of resources also decrees this ar-

rangement; the white community needs its most dedicated
and capable hands, hearts, and minds to achieve its own
internal readjustments.

In addition to the more obvious forms of interracial
communication, there are other important ways in which
Americans are engaged as a whole people. Reactions to
the processes of law—including acceptance and challenge
—represent a form of dialogue that we must come to accept as natural and therapeutic, especially because relationships with law will become more and more central as
we come to grips with continuing change.

What we see now as disruptions, involving mass protest,
actually represent part of the law-making process that has
been continuous in every society. In a semistatic society
such disruptions can be absorbed without too great pain.
But, as rapid civic and technological change becomes a
major part of our lives, elementary good sense should predispose us to deal as creatively as possible with the inevitable. Rapid and continuing change will mean the
emergence of increasing numbers of amorphous and constantly realigning minorities who sense that society affords
them no equity and that our society in particular no longer
serves their fundamental human needs. These groups, if
not dealt with creatively by responsible citizens and
groups, will disrupt or bring to an end the system that
effectively excludes them.

If the sense of alienation or exclusion is not too great,
only temporary disruption, of the kind represented by the
Poor People's Campaign in the spring of 1968, will result.
The purpose of such a campaign was communication across
race lines in two senses: It was itself a biracial campaign,
and it was addressed to a white-controlled Congress on
behalf of primarily black people. As a form of "extralegal"
participation in the democratic legislative process, it is
part of a long tradition of proved value. The suffragettes,
the veterans, the labor unions, and the original signers of

the Declaration of Independence all participated in activities not unlike this campaign, and such efforts will occur with accelerating frequency in the days ahead. Unless our society prepares itself for continuing adjustment, these confrontations may so sharply polarize our people as to rend our nation asunder.

In this sense, the leaders of present peaceable black protests may afford the nation a precious opportunity to prepare itself—while there is still time—to deal in positive ways with the recurrent stresses that are certain to lie ahead. At present black demands are overwhelmingly for entry into the system. Their "message" is low-keyed but insistent. If their voices are not heard and the nation continues to react in an arrogant and repressive way, however, attempts at communication may take on a more strident character, and the black voices of discontent may be joined—as evidence already suggests—by *non*black voices, such as those heard in the student revolts.

Responsible men and women, both black and white and of every political persuasion, must therefore join forces to create an appropriate atmosphere and revise legislative machinery for a far more efficient response to the rapidly changing requirements of providing equity for all in our society.

The basic goals of the Poor People's Campaign must be recognized as the minimal requirements for a humane society. The guarantee of an economic floor beneath all our citizens, to enable them to survive with elementary human dignity, should appeal to conservatives and liberals alike. It would bring with it the elimination of most of the costly and dehumanizing machinery of our present system of public welfare. Its only possible danger is in the timing of its challenge to those who uphold the tradition of self-reliance in our nation. It would be tragic if these measures were taken too late for those who have long believed in this tradition to imbue our whole society with its spirit.

The nation finds itself today upon a plateau but one in which opportunity is inherent. If we can work together to make certain that the nation heeds the low-keyed, positive voices of those who presently seek equity in the system, we may prepare ourselves to continue on an upward journey. If we fail to grasp this opportunity, surely mounting strains in the future will bring us closer to disaster.

We must hear and recognize the discordant cries of anguish as efforts to communicate. Those among us who have ears to hear must alert others to hear and to respond. We must all come to understand that, just as those in our own households sometimes cry out: "I hate you! I hate you!"—meaning, "Why don't you love me any more?"— so current cries of repudiation represent despair among people still amenable to being received as members with equity in our society.

White people who would share in the accelerated communication called for by the urgency of our times should now support more than ever before the existing interracial organizations. They should also develop caucuses parallel to black caucuses as a further means of increasing communication on national, state, and local levels and within public and private agencies.

Essential to such an endeavor are setting of priorities and maximum leadership, at least for the present, by black people. Our immediate ability and willingness to adapt ourselves to make an effective response to elementary demands for equity for black people may test our capacity to adjust to the certain and far greater strains that lie immediately ahead.

Commitment to Self-Determination

Shortly after the release of the major reports on civil disorders in the spring of 1968, James Farmer wrote in *Civil Disobedience* (1968; italics added):

> Most current analyses of the black rebellions sweeping the cities of the nation have concentrated upon superficials. They have searched for the answers in terms of more and better houses in the ghettos, more jobs and better schools. Obviously, these things are desperately needed and would make life more tolerable for ghetto dwellers. I am convinced, though, that most of these analyses do not even grasp the fundamental nature of the problem. The implied question asked by such an analysis is what have "we" failed to give that "they" want? Have we shown too little paternalism? Must we give more, and if so, in what areas? . . . "Bread alone" is not the answer. The problem goes much deeper. . . .
>
> *In practical terms what the rebels are revolting against is their lack of control over their own lives.* They feel purchased, possessed, and exploited. The houses, stores, and institutions are owned by others. They lack the economic and political leverages to effect change. They lack self-determination. They see their community as being akin to a colony. Theirs is a colonial revolt. It is revolt against economic, cultural, and social imperialism. Hence, the slogan Black Power becomes all the more meaningful, as an aspiration and a goal.

The issue raised by the black rebellions must be recognized by those who would work across racial lines as having broad implications for the future of our society.

It is the deeply significant issue of self-determination. Freedom-loving men have through the ages given their lives for the right to control at least their immediate environments. It is this basic love of freedom that brought the masses of our people to these shores. Belatedly, to be sure, black Americans now seek to make the national dream of a "more perfect union" of men who cherish liberty above their own lives come true. All in our society who favor national rededication to the priority of freedom from excessive controls have, in their black fellow Americans, a formidable ally.

The hour is growing late for those who would extend and preserve a diversity that can enrich our nation of many peoples. Those who today seek reasonable and realistic "local control" are speaking for the kind of community or local integrity and responsibility that for generations enhanced the nation's greatness. Central and local control must always be in tension, but one cannot heavily dominate the other. Otherwise, we lose far too much that is precious in our common life.

All Americans need one another. Today black Americans are in the vanguard of the fight for self-determination and freedom from undue centralization and paralyzing bureaucratic control. Black people must be astute enough to ally their immediate interest in ending their exploitation by those outside their community with the immediate interest of other Americans in achieving freedom from excessive centralization. But it must be remembered that political coalitions are most effective when limited to short-term ends. Power wanes when such relationships are taken for granted.

The continual creation of new alliances for the achievement of positive ends will enrich the nation as it extends the process of mutual support so essential to the maintenance of a dynamic, fluid, and healthy national unity. It will serve to bring all the elements of our society into recurrent interplay, with the attendant development of new and enriching relationships. To see any segment of our people as a permanent or natural adversary is inimical to the internal cohesion of the nation.

The will for maximum control over one's own destiny is a mark of humanity. A humane society will commit itself to work aggressively to extend and preserve the opportunity for all its citizens to grow into fulfillment in self-directed ways. What we must work for, as an early step in interracial response to the needs of the despairing black urban masses, is the extension of authentic black-community control over as much of its environment as possible.

This step will carry our interracial efforts in two directions. It will mean, on one hand, the creation of local inventories by which we may recognize and work to eliminate every undue "outside" control that tends to "colonialize" black people. It will mean, on the other hand, strengthening the black community itself—which has been fractured by historical circumstances under white American control—in the development of unifying mechanisms (like those described in chapter 6) necessary for group power.

Interracial and racial groups may work in parallel ways to bring about the needed legislation to permit essential local involvements and responsibilities in our schools and elsewhere in our society. Schools function most efficiently when the success of their students is tied up with the personal security and self-esteem of their teachers. Teachers who feel relationship with their pupils will find personal satisfaction in the accomplishments of their students, even in colleges, where teachers teach best when the school spirit is that of a family and where there is a pervading sense that the students are in some way "our kind." This spirit accounts also for much of the success of Roman Catholic schools.

Local control is a reasonable goal. When the day comes that "outsiders" act and think as "insiders," the definition "local" will become all-inclusive. Until that day, however, the local people themselves—and their children—who are currently viewed as outsiders in the very schools that are, or should be, in the deepest sense their own, must control these schools for themselves.

Local police and courts must also be responsive to local needs. The primary purpose of all law-enforcement agencies must be viewed not as the negative one of exacting penalties but as the positive one of facilitating equitable and harmonious relations among our citizens. In small communities law-enforcement agencies most often serve as the friend of the people. The same spirit must somehow come to prevail in our cities.

While working for desegregation, interracial groups should also encourage black political, cultural, and economic development as part of black self-determination. This task may involve the discouragement, for a time at least, of substantial dispersion of black groups into the suburbs. Black people need power bases from which to command the resources to meet their continuing needs. Interracial groups, for precisely this reason, should concentrate first on developing broadly based metropolitan-area coalitions for black group power rather than upon program needs that will recur.

People who have power may be disliked, but they will always be respected. Dr. Farmer writes:

> . . . [R]acism can be checkmated by power, its incubus neutralized. In the real world of men's affairs, one does not have to love in his heart of hearts to deal with me. Antisemites will deal with Jews, union busters will bargain with labor. Haters will negotiate and bargain with a people if the hated have the capacity to impose sanctions.

Without power, black people are at the mercy of the decision-makers. With power, we must be reckoned with.

Equitable power relations, in which all our citizens participate significantly in the control of their own fortunes, are necessary for the good of all. Such relations will enhance the cause of liberty and self-reliance and help to restore, or build, the mutual respect that is an essential foundation stone for a free and humane society.

Planning for Urban Needs

Those who are concerned with cooperation between black and white people in work for urban peace and regeneration should understand some of the essential elements in planning for urban life. All of us are or will be involved to some degree in urban planning, if at no other level than contributing money or voting for leaders committed to certain approaches. It is important, therefore, for all of us to have at least some useful elementary insights.

Urban problems basically are not generated in the childhood environment of our cities. Problems come upon cities chiefly by addition or accretion through the adult environment. In our cities, we must almost always begin with the needs of adults if we are to go to the source of human problems. Michael Duffey, the twelve-year-old son of Professor Joseph Duffey of Hartford, Connecticut, offered an insight into urban problems that many professional planners lack. One evening when I was visiting in Hartford, I gave young Michael an urban-related problem. I made the statement that people who live in suburban communities tend to be intelligent, healthy, responsible, and highly self-directed and that people who live in cities tend to be the opposite.

Michael asked me whether or not the statement was really true. I explained that it was true in a generalized sense and that all social-scientific statements are generalizations from statistical trends. Then I asked young Michael to try to figure out why people living in the city tended to be different from those living in the suburbs.

Michael thought for a moment. Then he came up with a marvelous, yet elementary, observation that should be illuminating to a good many people. He reasoned that, if a person were born blind in one of the suburban communities around Hartford, that person would best spend his adult life in downtown Hartford, for there would be— among other things—fewer walking patterns to memorize for a larger number of needed services.

Michael Duffey had begun to figure out a problem that so many governmental and other agencies have ignored. We send our problem adults from the suburbs into the city: the ill, the subnormal, and all others who do not fit into suburban life for one reason or another. This process gives much of the basic shape to the peculiar problems of urban life. Because it is as adults that these people bring their problems to our cities, we must focus our urban planning primarily upon the rehabilitation and development needs of adults.

When we are asked, then, to lend our aid or moral support to urban projects, if we wish to put first things first, we shall be emphatic in our concern that adult needs come first. Ideally adults should be in a position to plan and provide for their own children's needs. Admittedly, this solution does require more of what some call "grit and gumption" than does work with children. But reasonable and responsible men and women tackle problems not chiefly because they are easy but because they are the right problems to face. Our serious times can afford an attitude no less sensible.

There are at least several critical areas in which we

may work together to meet pressing urban needs of black adults in such a way as to improve, both quickly and significantly, the lives of all.

Economic Needs

Urban black people who would escape a sense of stultifying powerlessness must control local economic resources. Development funds should be built up from interracial sources for the purchase of businesses in black communities. These businesses should be purchased chiefly by black cooperatives as a ready means for involving black people in the prevailing economic system. Such cooperatives must be encouraged and helped toward success. Still their long-range success is not as important as the immediate benefit of dealing a largely dispossessed people in at the ownership level of our capitalistic system. Cooperatives represent capitalism minus exploitation. The persistence of businesses operated by "outsiders"—who have been at the very least the symbols of exclusion, exploitation, and oppression—should for the time being be discouraged. Black people need immediate evidence of freedom from economic exploitation. Those from whom businesses are purchased should make reasonable profits, however good or bad their past experiences may have been. Some individual enterprise must also be encouraged. But the safety and peace of our cities cannot withstand the impact of mere substitution of one exploiter for another.

The black community has tremendous residual economic power, which, if put to work for the community's own benefit, will begin to provide black people with an equitable stake in the nation's life and move our cities far closer to peace and economic stability. Albert Black, the tireless chairman of Newark's Commission on Human Rights and Vice-President of Newark's Management Associates, tells of the latent economic power among black people. It simply awaits an urgently needed catalyst to redirect it for the black community's benefit. Here are some of the facts on black economics in New Jersey as spelled out by Mr. Black in the April 13, 1968, issue of the *New Jersey Afro-American:*

> This alert, sensitive group spends $3,750,000 daily for an amazing variety of consumer needs, yet has not and does not utilize its tremendous purchasing power as a constructive force against reactionary economic forces. . . .
>
> The black man has failed to recognize the fact that his purchasing power has kept the existing economic power structure strong, wealthy and secure while he struggles to exist on a sub-standard level.
>
> These figures, as enlightening as they may be, become quite disheartening when one notes that the black person in New Jersey spends $293,568,000 for food yet does not own or control one supermarket and it is doubtful, throughout the state, if one half dozen black managers of supermarkets can be found.
>
> He spends $211,200,000 for clothing yet there is not one large clothing store owned or operated by black people. And how many of the large clothing stores have black people at the executive and policy making level?
>
> He spends $31,680,000 for furniture, yet there is not one major furniture store in New Jersey owned or controlled by black people.
>
> He spends more for alcoholic beverages ($52,800,-000) than he does for furniture ($31,680,000), cosmetics ($31,680,000) or fuel ($42,240,000).
>
> Of the hundreds of package liquor stores in Essex County it would be difficult to find three colored owners, yet black patrons spend 22 million dollars

annually in Essex County alone for beer, whiskey and wine.

Throughout the state of New Jersey, he spends $52,800,000 on alcoholic beverages. Of the 600 odd taverns in Newark less than 8 percent of them are owned by colored people.

These figures are not only disturbing and appalling, but they are tragic. . . .

He spends $79,200,000 for household goods and appliances yet does not own one major appliance store in New Jersey.

He spends $211,200,000 per year on insurance, education and savings yet it is very questionable how much of this amount is channelled back into this community.

Black people have economic potential. But their long exclusion from the benefits of our economic machinery has done much to predispose them toward alienation and immobilization. A cooperative effort must be made to afford to black people *full control* of economic resources in the black community. Furthermore, every effort must be made at the same time to begin to involve black people equitably in the economic life of the general community. Nothing short of such efforts will enable black people to overcome the handicap of business exploitation over the years. This step and far more may be necessary to save our cities from mounting alienation and a growing challenge to the economic system itself, as it appears more and more to be simply a white-controlled instrument for black oppression.

The work of the Interracial Council for Business Opportunity and numerous black-initiated endeavors for economic development should be given interracial support. Even more important, new and more effective interracial efforts should be made toward the fullest use of black skills in every area of our economic life. Sooner or later it must be understood that simple justice requires extended or intermittent moratoria on the employment of other than black people in order to overcome the handicap built up over a period of generations. That white America, which unduly controls power, has discriminated against black America is clear on every hand. Recognition of this fact alone should suggest some reassessment of our total economic endeavors with an eye toward equity and restitution in partial economic justice to black people.

Educational Needs

That all our people should be made economically productive and capable of enjoying life is a reasonable goal for a society that claims to be humane. It is implicit when we speak of liberty and prosperity for all.

For the fast-approaching day of shorter periods of more technical work and longer periods of leisure, a vastly different system of education must be developed. It must be oriented toward full realization of life. It must be rewarding. It must relate to realities. It must "turn people on," lead them out, as one meaning of "education" (from the Latin *e-ducere*) suggests.

A critical aspect of education as it relates to urban peace, one to which interracial attention must be given, is the re-entry into the educational process of the aimless, hopeless army of understandably angry black youth in our cities. It is from among this army that our black fire bombers emerge. Yet their very knack for survival in a hostile and alien world testifies to their ingenuity, initiative, and capacity to achieve. On every hand there is evidence that their apparent "failure" is actually a combination of our incapacity and our unwillingness to inspire and relate to these incalculably valuable young people, the waste of whose talents represents a tragic drain on our nation's resources and places our very survival in jeopardy.

These young people—for the present—can and must be reclaimed chiefly by black institutions of higher learning. The Office of Economic Opportunity and other public and private agencies should begin a high-priority infusion of substantial funds into those black institutions that are predisposed to become black "multiversities"—as Shaw University and Benedict College most notably have demonstrated a willingness to do—adopting a thoroughly developmental approach, vital for all higher education.

Those black youths who are attending northern white colleges on "crash" programs are, by and large, as many have observed, angry. They are said to be compromised and used by institutions that, like our racist society as a whole, do not perceive black people as persons. There are notable exceptions; for example, at least one white institution that seeks large numbers of black students is opening top administrative and teaching posts to black people. In most instances, however, white institutions continue to be dominated by white purposes yet expect at the same time to serve the needs of black urban youth. The opposite expectation is more valid. In their "business as usual" attitude, in their structural power relations, these institutions are alienating our black youths and provoking and abetting them in their attitude of either "in also for us" or "out, indeed, for all."

Interracial groups may organize local corporations to identify and recruit large numbers of these black youths for re-entry into the educational system. Funds should be used to deal with this problem on a large scale. Angry and destructive today, tomorrow these young people will be an even greater burden and a surer threat to us all if nothing is done. Is there a choice other than to act with determination and purpose?

Political Needs

We must work interracially to achieve equity in our political system for black people. As noted earlier, such enterprises as urban renewal and "drop-outism" work to depoliticize black people. But people who *feel* powerless act as if they are. The consequences for society are severe. In fact many processes combine to deny black people actual political power.

The political powerlessness of black people must be assessed from at least two points of view: It has worked against the efficient reconstruction of our cities and has entrenched an arbitrary rule that is not in the public interest from any angle. The inability of black people to function with political effectiveness is also a symptom of a growing disease in our society as a whole, the inability of majorities generally to rule effectively. The condition of black people presents us all with a strategic opportunity now to reverse the trend away from arbitrary rule to the just rule of the majority in the reasonable interest of all. "With a federal budget of $425 millions for public relations," writes Paul Goodman, "democratic choice becomes almost impossible." Mr. Goodman also notes that, beyond the immediate reach of the ballot, "There is a 'hidden government' of CIA and FBI."

Those who value liberty and who would preserve and extend just rule should work together to reverse our present course. The facilitation of political equity for black people may be our best present opportunity to restore government to the point at which it represents in a reasonable way "the will of the people."

Interracial groups may give political support to black candidates for public office, as in Newark, where black people constitute more than a 60 per cent majority and a 70 per cent majority in the schools. Yet the school board has only three black members out of nine and has an administrative and teaching staff that does not "relate," in the sense we have recently noted, to the basic circumstances of the students. The results are predictable: "There isn't anyone who can say in the city of Newark, professional or otherwise, we are doing a good job," says Harold Ashby, President of the Newark Board of Education, "because these children just can't read and do arithmetic." Black people in Newark hold two positions out of seven on the housing authority, whose work is so vital to the black community's needs. There are two black councilmen out of seven, and most of the boards of city control have only token black members if any. A black deputy mayor, a former athlete who has engaged in public relations, was appointed in the spring of 1968.

Interracial groups in cities throughout the country should aid black people to achieve the political participation and control they deserve. Black people should not be coalesced out of political effectiveness in such a process. Enduring alliances cannot be usefully formed before black men have a solid power base. There are, however, places where black men even now have the power to ally themselves with others. This power has been demonstrated in Gary, Indiana, and Cleveland, Ohio. Black mayors have also been elected in smaller predominantly white cities.

Black people need the Senator Edward Brookes and the Justice Thurgood Marshalls to pave the way. They do not expect these men, in every case, to be primarily black-oriented. Some must blend to a degree into the white American landscape. This, too, is power, as both Manhattan Borough President Percy Sutton and Michigan's U.S. Representative John Conyers have often emphasized. But all of these men would agree that the fundamental need throughout the nation is for black people as a group to develop authentic and enduring political power. The development of such power will serve to reverse the current trend away from representative government and will thus benefit the entire nation. James Farmer writes, "If black people can bring into the nation's life the new ingredient of popular participation, the wielding of levers of real decision-making and power by the hitherto excluded, they will have transformed America."

Cultural Needs

The positive values of our black American subculture must be incorporated by black people as a whole and then shared with the nation as a whole. Interracial groups may work to achieve this end in several ways. Such groups should affirm the need for black solidarity and black self-awareness, and in rejoicing at the gifts or values that black people may share with the nation they must be careful not to corrupt their development. Interracial groups are needed at this juncture, and so are racial groups.

Dr. George Kent of Quinnipiac College in Hamden, Connecticut, suggests how black ethnic values may be taught in college courses. His remarks are made in an article entitled "Ethnic Impact in American Literature: Reflections on a Course" (CLA *Journal*, Vol. XI, September 1967). Some key values prominent in black folk literature are, as Dr. Kent explains:

1. The insistence upon a tough-minded grip upon reality.
2. A willingness to confront the self, searchingly and even with laughter.
3. Patience and endurance.
4. Humor as a tool for transcendence.
5. A sort of deadend courage, and not so deadend.
6. An acceptance of the role of suffering in retaining one's humanity and in retaining some perspective on the humanity of the oppressor.

7. A high development of dissimulation and camou-
   flage.
8. A sense of something more than this world and of
   its rhythms.
9. A deep sense of the inexorable limitations of life
   and all that we associate with the tragic and
   tragicomic vision.
10. Ceremonies of poise in a nonrational universe
    (the hipsters and the cool-cats play an endless
    satire upon Western assumptions of rationality).
    (p. 30)

Interracial groups may listen to black people. They may
listen and learn, and they may help others to listen. They
may encourage the black man to go alone into the desert,
as all men who would be mature and wise must do from
time to time, that his retreat and self-examination may
result in new resources for the transformation of us all.

Some men make history. Others simply follow it. In
perilous times if we follow the followers we are soon lost.
Our times call for men, women, and perhaps especially
young people who will work to chart a new day by firmly
setting aside the shibboleths of the past and by looking
openly toward the future sure of but one thing: Those
whose eyes are cast backward are lost.

Far too many among us already *feel* that our nation
and its institutions no longer hold any promise of serving
their basic needs. The disaffected include alarmingly increasing numbers on grounds other than race. Whether
our society will ever again become legitimate or viable in
their eyes depends chiefly upon the openness of those who
wish to preserve America and to make it once more into
a land of hope and opportunity for all.

Two quotations remind us far better than any words I
might write here of our need to work together in every

possible way. The first is by Laurence M. Gould, President Emeritus of Carleton College.

> I do not believe the greatest threat to our future is from bombs or guided missiles. I don't think our civilization will die that way. I think it will die when we no longer care. Arnold Toynbee has pointed out that nineteen of twenty-one civilizations have died from within and not by conquest from without. There were no bands playing and flags waving when these civilizations decayed. It happened slowly, in the quiet and the dark when no one was aware.

The other is the late Langston Hughes' "Dream Deferred":

> What happens to a dream deferred?
>
> Does it dry up
> like a raisin in the sun
> Or fester like a sore—
> And then run?
> Does it stink like rotten meat?
> Or crust and sugar over—
> like a syrupy sweet?
>
> Maybe it just sags
> like a heavy load.
>
> Or does it explode? *

Let's work together—for peace and power for all!

* From Langston Hughes, *The Panther and the Lash: Poems for Our Times* (New York: Knopf, 1967).

Index

259